the story of

ILLUSTRATED BY KATHLEEN ELGIN

Some Other Books by Mary Elting

The Answer Book
The Lollypop Factory
The First Book of Nurses
We Are the Government
Trucks at Work
Trains at Work
Ships at Work
Machines at Work
The Helicopter Mystery (*Fiction*)
Patch (*Fiction*)
Wishes and Secrets *Fiction*)

Some Other Books by Franklin Folsom

Exploring American Caves (*For adults*)
Explorations of America
The First Book of Indians (*Pseudonym*,
     Benjamin Brewster)
The First Book of Eskimos (*Pseudonym*,
     Benjamin Brewster)
The Real Book About Indians
     (*Pseudonym*, Michael Gorham)
The Real Book of Great American Jour-
     neys (*Pseudonym*, Michael Gorham)
Beyond the Frontier (*Fiction*)
The Hidden Ruin (*Fiction*)
Search in the Desert (*Fiction*)
Sand Dune Pony Mystery (*Fiction*)
Mystery at Rustlers' Fort (*Fiction*)

HARVEY HOUSE, PUBLISHERS •

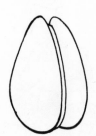

1

ARCHEOLOGY
in the Americas

BY

MARY ELTING AND FRANKLIN FOLSOM

Reviewed for Scientific Accuracy by
J. Alden Mason, Ph.D., Curator Emeritus
American Section
The University Museum of the University of Pennsylvania

HARVEY HOUSE, PUBLISHERS
Irvington-on-Hudson, New York

A Story of Science Series Book for Young People

HARVEY HOUSE, PUBLISHERS
Irvington-on-Hudson, New York

Library of Congress Catalog Card No.: 60-9437

Manufactured in the United States of America
December 1960

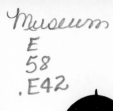

Contents

1

The Cliff Dweller Mystery

Richard Wetherill was a cowboy in the old West. He was a detective, too — a special kind of detective. While he trailed after missing steers on the range in southern Colorado, he also searched for clues to missing people. These people had vanished long, long before Richard was born. But they had left a good many of their belongings scattered around. Some had lived in dry caves, and there Richard found their baskets, pottery dishes, stone tools, arrowheads.

Who *were* the makers of these things? Could they have been the ancestors of the Ute Indians who lived near by?

Richard questioned one of his Ute friends.

The Indian answered positively, "No!" The vanished people were the Old Ones, he said, and he knew nothing at all about them. But he suspected that their spirits might bring bad luck to anyone who disturbed the caves where they had made their homes.

Richard kept wondering about the Old Ones, the lost tribe that nobody could explain. Then, one winter day in 1888, he and his cousin Charley Mason came upon an amazing sight. From the edge of a cliff they peered down across a wild, lonely canyon, and there in the opposite cliff wall they saw a whole village crowded into a cave. Houses made of stone filled the long opening. A round tower and a square one rose almost to the cavern roof.

No smoke came from any of the buildings this chilly afternoon. There were no children shouting and playing in the snow. Not a soul stirred. What had happened here? Where had the inhabitants gone? Why? Had they left any treasure behind?

The two cowboys decided to visit the cave and find out.

The quickest way seemed to be down the face of the cliff. Richard and Charley proceeded to make a ladder — the kind of ladder the Old Ones, themselves, had often used. They broke branches from a couple of fallen trees. Then, with their lariats they lashed the top of one tree to the bottom of the other. The combined height of the two trunks was enough to reach from the rim of the cliff to a landing place far below. Down this unsteady ladder the cousins went, using the stumps of broken branches as footholds and handholds. Across the canyon bottom, up a slope, and there they were, exploring a ghost-town-in-a-cave.

The cousins poked into room after room. Everywhere they saw things that looked as though the owners had just gone out for a while and expected to return. Big jars, which had surely held water long ago, waited beside doorways to be filled again at the nearby spring. Soot-blackened cooking pots stood amid bits of charred wood, as if the dead embers might burst into flame any moment.

The Real Story

The more Richard looked, the more he wanted to know. What was the real story of this town? What were the stories of the other towns he was to discover in neighboring canyons? What kind of people had lived here in caves in the cliff walls, along the sides of canyons? What had made these cliff dwellers leave their snug well-built homes?

No one in the world could answer those questions in the year 1888. The forgotten villages in the caves were a baffling mystery. But Richard kept on looking for clues. So did others who visited the cliffs

The ancient people who lived here needed the stone wall along their front yard to keep them from falling down a seven-hundred-foot cliff.

and canyons. Bit by bit the mystery was solved — at least, much of it was solved. Today, you can go and see for yourself the ghost town that Richard and his cousin discovered in the cave. He named it Cliff Palace, and it is part of Mesa Verde (MAY-sah-VERD) National Park. What is more, in the museum at the Park, you can find out how Cliff Palace looked when people still lived there.

A Ruin Comes to Life

This is part of Cliff Palace on an autumn day about seven hundred years ago. The little boy at the left carries a bow and arrow for a man who has just killed a rabbit. The hunter will skin the rabbit carefully and save the fur to use in making a warm winter robe. His wife is getting ready to fix rabbit stew for dinner. She is pouring water from her water jar into a black cooking pot beside the fire. Along with stew she will serve corn bread. The bread will be made from meal that the women in the family grind by hand. You can see two of them

at work beside the tower. They are crushing and grinding the corn kernels between stones.

The large round hole at the far right is going to be a combination church and club room for some of the men. When it is finished, the room will be entirely underground. It will have a ceiling of poles which the man with the stone axe has been cutting.

The turkeys that wander about the yard will not end up in any Thanksgiving feast. At Cliff Palace a turkey lives a long and sheltered life. (On page 28 you will find out why.)

Detectives at Work

Perhaps you are wondering if the picture of Cliff Palace is a true one. Did things really happen this way?

They did indeed. And they are only a tiny part of a very big picture that could be drawn. But how can we be sure? Has somebody discovered books that these Old Ones left behind, and did the books tell the story?

No, the Old Ones left no books. They had none to leave. Knowledge of how to write had not reached them.

The story of the cliff dwellers was pieced together in exactly the way a detective solves a mystery. First, it was necessary to gather many, many facts. But instead of just one expert like Sherlock Holmes working on the case, dozens of clever men and women hunted for clues. These experts are archeologists, and they can track down missing facts in ways that would astonish Holmes, himself.

After an archeologist has his evidence, he tries to figure out what it all means. He decodes messages from forgotten men who spoke forgotten tongues. He becomes a voice for human beings who cannot talk about themselves.

As a rule an archeologist has to learn about people by studying *things*. He digs into dust and dirt, and saves every scrap that he finds — including ancient garbage. Sometimes, he shovels out earth and

14

sifts it through a screen which catches broken pottery or bones or hammers or seeds or beads. In a very dry cave he may have to wear a dust mask. Often he digs carefully with a small trowel, taking great pains not to break anything fragile. He may use even finer tools, such as a small soft paint brush or a little bellows to blow dust out of the way. If he finds bones that are soft and crumbly, he coats them with model airplane dope, a liquid plastic. The dope gives them strength when it hardens. Occasionally he has to poke and pry with the same tool a dentist uses when he hunts for cavities in your teeth!

The archeologists who investigated the cliff dwellings soon discovered other mysterious villages near by in Arizona, New Mexico and Utah. Sometimes they were in caves, sometimes not. But always, the inhabitants had vanished.

What had become of all these people? Archeologists asked the Navaho Indians. But the Navahos had no clues. They merely said that the villages once belonged to the Anasazi (ah-nah-SAH-zee), which is their word for Old Ones. Anasazi seemed a handy name, and archeologists began to use it.

Mysterious Rooms

A ruin, even one that seems to have nothing left in it, can be full of strange possibilities. The rooms of many cliff dwellings, for instance, are very small. Only very short people could stand up in them. Does this prove that the cliff dwellers were small? Watch out before you jump to that conclusion. When an archeologist studies a ruin he examines everything — walls, ceilings, doors, floors, and secret rooms whose doors have been sealed shut.

15

Suppose you found the skeleton of a man who had been buried in a sealed-up room in a cliff dwelling. You could certainly measure the bones to see whether they proved that the Old Ones were very small people. Archeologists did measure many cliff dweller skeletons. And what did they learn? They discovered that the Old Ones were rather short people, but not short enough to stand upright in their own houses!

The puzzle grows less puzzling if you visit a cliff village on a rainy day. You will see that the Old Ones did not need big rooms where whole families could spend their time in wet weather. The roof of the cave, itself, kept them dry. People cooked and ate, worked and played out of doors. They did sleep inside, but a low ceiling was no inconvenience when they were lying down.

There was another unusual thing about the cliff dwellers' houses. Many had doorways shaped like the letter T, broad at the top and narrow at the bottom. Why?

Archeologists made some guesses, and then they tried an experiment. A T-shaped door, they discovered, is very good for entering a low room. You put your hands on the little ledges at either side of the door. Then, resting your weight on your hands, you swing yourself

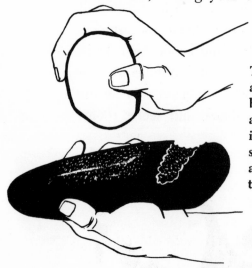

This is how an Old One made an axe. He selected a hard stone worn smooth by water. A stream bed was a good place to look for it. Using another stone as a hammer, he pecked away at it until he had the shape he wanted. Then he sharpened the blade by rubbing it against still another stone. He made the handle from a green tree branch.

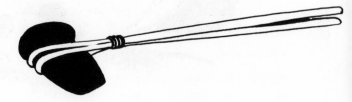

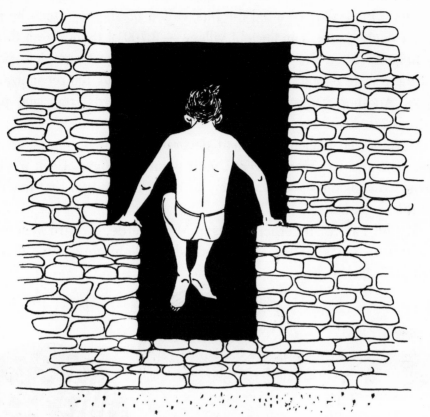

into the room with feet doubled up under you, and you land in a squatting position. A smart way to keep from bumping your head!

The more the experts learned about the Old Ones' houses, the surer they were that Richard Wetherill had given the wrong name to Cliff Palace. A palace is the home of a king or a rich noble. It is much grander than the homes of common people. But the Old Ones' houses were all alike. The empty little rooms in Cliff Palace say clearly that the people who lived here shared equally whatever they had.

Slues of Clues

Bowls and jars and pots that the Old Ones left in their homes add another chapter to the story. Explorers and archeologists found some of the pots unbroken. They also dug up thousands and thousands of shattered pieces which they patiently fitted together until they could tell how the ancient dishes or jars had looked, and what they had been used for. One expert counted the bits, called *potsherds*, which he got from a single house in an ancient village — 2,700 of them. From these, his helpers sorted out enough to make eight almost complete pots, and there were enough left over to make more than 400 recognizable dishes. Another archeologist took 108,305 potsherds from one part of one trash heap!

Most of the ancient pots had decorations. Bowls, plates, mugs, dippers, water jars were covered with painted designs. Even a soot-blackened cooking vessel was likely to have little ridges that made it look like a basket.

At Cliff Palace and other places in Mesa Verde, Richard Wetherill saw velvety black patterns on hundreds of light-gray pots. This is what they looked like:

These bowls came from another village, which is about a week's walk south of Cliff Palace. Can you tell the difference?

18

Mimbres Pots

The plates above came from still another village farther south, near the Mimbres (MIMM-bress) River.

Of course you can see how different these pots are. In ancient times, almost every village had its own special kinds of decoration, even its own favorite shapes and colors for pots. If you learn to recognize these special styles, you can tell which town a pot probably came from!

But suppose you dig into a room at Mesa Verde and find a dish that looks like a dish from some other town. This has indeed happened to archeologists. Should it throw a pottery detective off the track? Not at all. It adds something very interesting to his collection of facts. The mixed-up pottery means that somebody from Mesa Verde visited another town, liked the dishes there, and brought a sample home. Or, perhaps, a stranger came to Mesa Verde and exchanged his dish for food. Pottery tells us that these people travelled and traded throughout the ancient Southwest.

Fashions in Footwear

The Old Ones had fashions in sandals as well as in pots. Some people made their sandals from the long narrow leaves of a plant called yucca. Others used cotton cord. One kind of sandal was square and would fit either foot. Another kind was made in pairs with a definite shape for left and right foot. In some villages people wore full-length sandals, but in others they used scuffs which protected only the toes, leaving the heels bare.

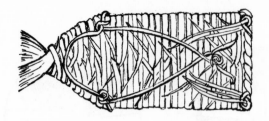
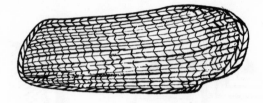

By looking at what men wore on their feet long ago, an expert today can usually tell from which part of the Southwest they came.

Suppose you discovered a cave where sandals were scattered all over the floor — hundreds and hundreds of them. What would it mean to you? Two archeologists, Mr. and Mrs. C. B. Cosgrove, found just such a cave. Was it the home of an ancient shoemaker? Maybe he kept a sort of store where he traded sandals for corn or blankets.

But wait a minute. Could the cave have been a second-hand store? The sandals in it had been worn. Some of them even had holes in the bottom. Most baffling of all, they showed that they had been made in many different villages. There were square toes and rounded toes, criss-cross lacings, fringes.

The Cosgroves did a lot of digging in this cave and in others near by, and they came up with a solution to the mystery. The cave of the sandals was a place of religious ceremonies. People had not made their homes in it, for they left no cooking pots or garbage scraps behind. Instead they left headdresses, used in religious dances, and little sticks with curious tassels — and sandals. The sticks were very much like things called prayer sticks which some Indians still use in ceremonies. Somehow this cave must have grown famous as a holy place. Many pilgrims from different villages went there to pray and to hold ceremonies. Afterward, the visitors left their sandals behind as religious offerings.

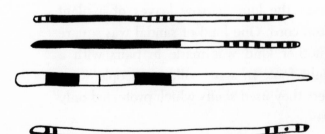

Prayer sticks made from wood or the stalks of desert flowers were left in Ceremonial Cave. People believed that a stick could carry a prayer to the gods if it was placed in a sacred spot.

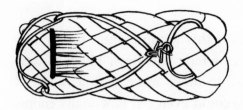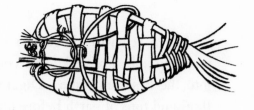

The caves were miles from the nearest Anasazi town, and the Cosgroves found no Anasazi sandals in it. Perhaps the Old Ones left *their* sandals somewhere else.

Beautiful Town

Visitors often went to ancient towns on business trips, too. A man who had sea shells from California could trade them in New Mexico for turquoise, the greenish-blue stone used in jewelry. Anyone with a pet parrot from the far-off jungles of Mexico could find a market for it among the Old Ones. Pueblo Bonito (PWAY-bloh boh-NEE-toh), the biggest of their towns, had a whole room that was used as one big parrot cage!

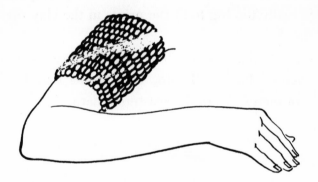

This bracelet made of seashells was found in the grave of an Old One many hundreds of miles from the sea. Shells and other precious things travelled great distances as people traded with each other.

Pueblo Bonito, of course, is a modern name. In Spanish the words mean Beautiful Town. Once it really was a place of beauty, but not when United States cavalrymen first discovered it more than a hundred years ago. It looked then like a huge mound of earth, with the tops of ruined stone walls showing above it.

21

When scientists began to excavate this mound, they had a tremendous job. For unknown centuries winds had been blowing dust into the deserted rooms. Diggers had to move more than a hundred thousand tons of earth before anyone could even tell how many rooms had been built there.

The scientists hired Zuni and Navaho Indians to help them. And what did they find at last? A town built like an apartment house, four stories high in places, with homes enough for twelve hundred people. Some of the stone walls had been laid up in beautiful patterns, finer than any in the neighboring towns and cliff dwellings. In many of the houses, adobe mud had been used as cement or plaster.

One thing about the plaster seemed strange to Neil Judd, the archeologist in charge of digging. The ancient masons had left the prints of their fingers on the mud, and those fingers had all belonged to small hands. Were the men at Pueblo Bonito very small?

"No," said the scientists when they found and measured the skeletons of Pueblo Bonito men. They were not particularly small. The hands were really too big to fit the prints in the clay plaster.

What then?

It turned out that the small fingerprints exactly fitted the hands of the *women* of Pueblo Bonito. This means that in the old times, women — not men — were the plasterers here.

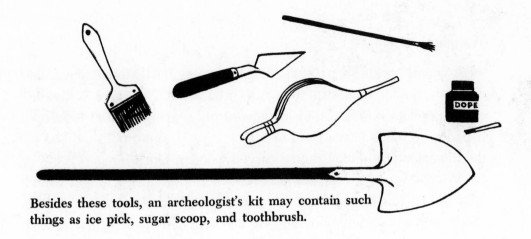

Besides these tools, an archeologist's kit may contain such things as ice pick, sugar scoop, and toothbrush.

What the Robbers Missed

One day Judd was doing some careful work in a room at Pueblo Bonito. Using a sharp trowel, he shaved the earth away in thin layers, and presently he saw a glint of something blue. Turquoise, he guessed it was — that lovely blue stone. The Old Ones treasured it, and Indians in the Southwest still regard it the way other people value diamonds. Many burial places at Pueblo Bonito had been opened by grave robbers looking for turquoise. But this was one grave they had missed.

Judd shaved off a little more earth with his trowel. More blue appeared — and more. At last he could see many turquoise beads, very tiny ones, still on an unbroken string, and the most beautiful shade of blue he had ever come across.

Word passed like magic around the big dusty ruin: the boss was uncovering a great treasure. Zuni and Navaho Indians dropped their tools quietly and edged over to the rickety ancient walls. Using a brush now, Judd pushed the dust aside from the beads and revealed not just a single string but four, joined together in one magnificent necklace.

In all there were 2500 tiny beads in the four strands. Some ancient jeweler had spent a great deal of time putting a hole in each tiny bead, then rubbing each one on a kind of whetstone until it exactly matched the others. Imagine how long it took to finish that four-strand necklace!

Trailing a Thief

A friend of Judd's, an archeologist named Earl Morris, once discovered another beautiful turquoise ornament in a grave. This one was a pendant which a man had worn on a string around his neck. It had been made in the form of a mosaic, with small polished bits of the blue stone cemented onto a carved wooden block.

Morris cleared away the dust from the mosaic, using a soft camel hair brush. Immediately he saw something odd. Three bits of the precious turquoise were missing. He knew *he* had not lost them, for he had been very careful. He also knew that in ancient times people buried the dead with only the very best jewelry. Surely a grave robber would have taken the whole thing, not just a small part of it. What then could explain this mosaic that lacked three stones?

Morris began a search. He noticed a mouse's tunnel in the ground near the spot where the ornament had been. He dug along the tunnel and sifted every spoonful of earth that came out. At last, the three missing bits of blue stone appeared. A mouse had been the grave robber.

Corn Gives a Clue

It took many days, more likely many weeks, for a man to do all the work of making a mosaic pendant or a small string of turquoise beads to hang around his neck. A woman needed hours of free time to paint a complicated design on a pot.

What do these facts tell an archeologist? Do they mean that the Old Ones liked beautiful things? Certainly. That some Old Ones were skilled craftsmen and good artists? Yes. What else? The beads and the mosaic and the lovely dishes prove that the Old Ones did not have to spend all their time in a struggle to get food. Some of them at least could do special work that produced no food at all.

How did these people manage to be well fed and still have time enough to make beautiful things?

Archeologists have found many clues to the answer, and some of the best clues come from graves — women's graves. The Old Ones had the custom of burying useful objects with a dead person. There can be no doubt about the reason for this. Many, many groups of people all over the world have believed that after they died they would need possessions again in a future life. The things to put in a grave, they thought, were the very things that the dead person had found useful when he was alive.

Something else turned up in the grave of one cliff dweller woman: a large basket of the kind that women used as knapsacks for carrying burdens on their backs. And in this basket lay the most useful of all burdens, ears of corn.

The corn proves that these cliff dwellers were farmers. Can we be quite sure of that? Maybe they just gathered wild corn.

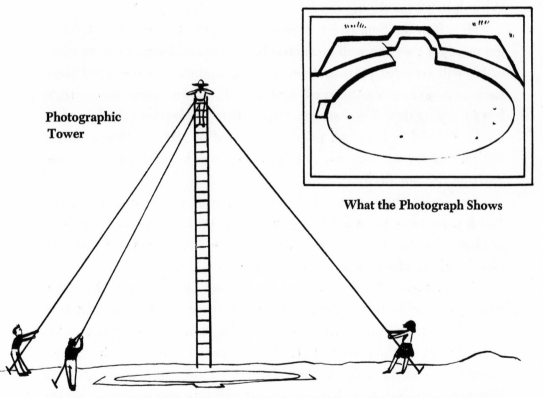

Photographic Tower

What the Photograph Shows

Often an archeologist wants to look straight down on a spot, and take a picture of it. A photograph may, for example, show him the outline of an ancient house that he would not notice if he were on level ground. This movable tower does the trick. The boys and girls are steadying the wires that hold the tower up.

Impossible. *Corn never grows wild.* People who want corn must plant it.

Corn in a woman's grave tells the archeologist a great deal. This woman did not depend on *finding* food. She and her people *created* food. By farming in the summer, they grew most of the food they needed for the whole year.

Corn gave the Old Ones leisure time for making pendants and necklaces and painted pots and many other beautiful things.

Precious Garbage

Does it surprise you that archeologists have found actual ears of corn many hundreds of years old? How could corn last all that time? Why didn't it spoil long ago?

The air in the Southwest is very dry, and most things do not rot or get moldy if they are well protected from rain and snow. Food or cloth or fur will keep for years and years in a container in a sheltered place such as a cave. Even the trash that the Old Ones threw away might last for a long time. Food scraps, torn clothes, broken toys, broken tools made of wood or bone, all piled up in front of cliff dwellings. And if the roof of the cave jutted out far enough to keep the rain off, the garbage did not decay.

You might think that all this trash is useless, nothing but junk. But it is precious to an archeologist. So are broken pots and even bits of charred wood. Here in the garbage heaps lies buried treasure — a rich supply of clues for a scientist to work on.

Not all trash piles stay dry, of course, not even those which *seem* to be sheltered by overhanging rock. But a bit of sleuthing usually tells an archeologist, even before he starts to dig, whether or not decay has been at work on the garbage in front of a cave. If grass and other plants cover the heap, he will probably have poor digging. Green growing things mean moisture in the soil — and moisture means decay. Where plants do not grow, there is no moisture in the soil, and a good chance that ancient treasures have been preserved.

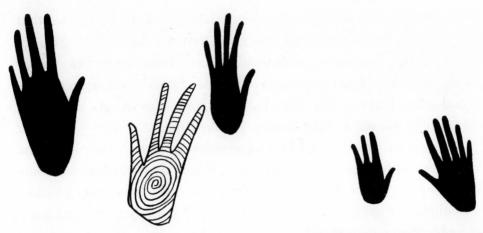

Paintings of hands decorated the wall of one Anasazi cave. They were real paintings, not just prints left by paint-smeared hands. You probably wonder why some of them have six fingers or four. Archeologists wonder, too.

Talking Bones

Bones in a trash pile — what do they tell? They may show what kind of meat the Old Ones ate. Rabbit bones mean rabbit meat. Deer bones, deer meat.

But that is only the beginning. Suppose an archeologist, just out of curiosity, assembles some broken deer bones that he finds in a dozen different houses in a village. The jagged edges mesh together. The bones fit one another like the pieces of a jigsaw puzzle. They all come from one deer!

Now the archeologist knows much more than the simple fact that the Old Ones liked deer meat. The bones have actually told him one of the rules that governed this village. The bones have said: "The people here shared things. If one had food, all ate." The archeologist adds this fact to the fact that all the rooms in the village are the same size, with no palaces for rulers. He feels more sure than ever that the Old Ones practiced democracy.

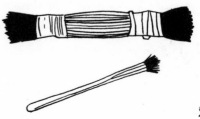

Anasazi Paint Brushes

27

Bones can also tell something very different. They can prove that the creature they came from was *not* eaten. In the ancient garbage heaps of the Southwest, archeologists have found very few turkey bones that show signs of being cooked or chewed. But diggers *have* found many turkeys that were buried whole. This means, of course, that people did not kill the turkeys for their meat.

Why, then, did the Old Ones keep turkeys at all? They grew the birds for the feathers! Every once in a while, they plucked out some of the feathers and used them in making warm blankets. After a turkey was plucked it grew a new crop of feathers. Naturally it was much too valuable for anyone to eat.

Tales That Dead Men Tell

A turkey-feather blanket was very useful in this life, and the Old Ones believed it woud be equally useful when a person went on to a future world. That is why the blankets are often found in burial places. Many a grave was dug in the loose dry material of the trash piles in front of the caves. Sometimes the bodies of the dead withered up and became mummies. A mummy wrapped in a feather blanket and surrounded by possessions can give an archeologist important clues. So can skeletons or sometimes even a few bones. On the next pages you will see some of these clues.

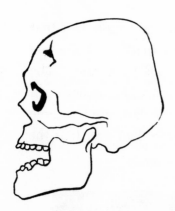

This skull is all that is left of a man who lived in Arizona more than a thousand years ago, but it is enough to tell a story about his life. (1) When he was a baby his mother wanted him to look fashionable. (2) As he grew up, he ate a great deal of corn bread, although it was sometimes difficult for him to chew because his teeth ached. (3) He was killed in an ambush. (4) He was about thirty-five years old when he died.

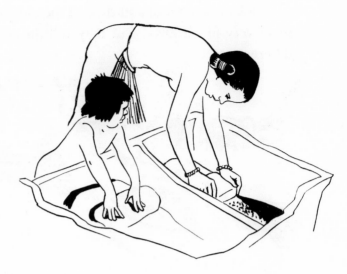

(1) **Fashionable Old Ones** had heads that were flat in the back. To shape a baby's head, a mother bound it snugly to the cradle which she carried on her back. The soft head bones soon flattened out and stayed flat after they grew hard.

(2) **Why did an Old One have bad teeth?** Sand got mixed into corn meal when women used sandstone grinding tools. Chewing on sandy corn bread day after day wore teeth down to stumps.

(3) **The position of the arrowhead,** with its tip showing in the forehead, makes us think that an enemy shot from *below*, so that the arrow entered beneath the ear and pierced the forehead from the inside.

(4) **Did the skull belong to a man or a woman?** Young or old? How old? Scientists have measured and studied so many skeletons that they can give us the answers.

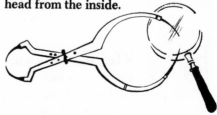

Look at this burial and then at the one on the opposite page. They seem very much alike. But they tell an archeologist two completely different stories.

Hairbrush

The bones, the hairbrush, and the polishing stone are some of the clues that tell a scientist, "This is a woman's grave." Like other Anasazi women she made pottery. After a pot was shaped, she smoothed it with a special polishing stone, then decorated it and baked it in a hot fire.

Polishing Stone

When she was a little girl, she broke her leg and had it bound in splints like this. A scientist can tell by studying the healed bone how old she was when the accident happened. Splints and crutches found in the Old Ones' trash heaps give further clues.

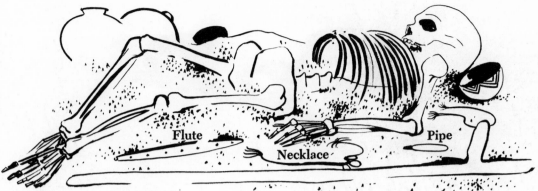

Flute

Necklace

Pipe

Digging Stick

We know that this is the grave of a man—an important man. Around him lie many pots of food and drink for a future life, several necklaces, and a flute. At ceremonies he sometimes played the flute and sometimes smoked a pipe that was just a straight hollow tube.

Like other Anasazi men, he hunted and worked in the field and planted his corn in deep holes that he made with a digging stick.

31

2

Older Than the Old Ones

After the cowboy Richard Wetherill discovered Cliff Palace in Colorado, he explored some caves in Arizona. Here he found something he had never seen before — egg-shaped graves in which bodies had been buried sitting upright. Often, he had to dig deep into the cave floor before he reached the burial holes. Richard began to suspect that the cliff dwellers had not known that the burials were there when they built their houses.

Another odd thing was this: the egg-shaped graves contained no pottery or arrowheads. All kinds of other useful things turned up — food, clothing, magnificent baskets, spear points. But Richard found none of the dishes and pots, or bows and arrows that the Old Ones usually buried with their dead. The sandals that he found in the egg-shaped graves were different, too. All the cliff-dweller sandals he knew about had a notch in the outside edge near the little toe. But here were sandals that had no notches or jogs.

The same puzzling facts appeared when Richard dug into the trash piles, too. The top layers had notched sandals and arrowheads. Farther down in the heaps there were plain sandals and spearheads but no arrowheads.

Did these differences mean anything? And if so, what? Richard felt sure they showed that, before the cliff dwellers, a very ancient people lived here. Before the Old Ones there were Older Ones.

All over the world, people have left rubbish where they lived. If people lived in the same spot for a long time, lots of rubbish piled up in layer after layer. And, of course, the newest was on the top and the oldest on the bottom.

By studying these layers of trash, scientists have figured out the order in which certain things happened. They know definitely, for example, that men used spears before they used bows and arrows. Baskets were invented before pottery. People lived on game and wild fruits and seeds before they grew corn.

The layers tell an archeologist which things happened first. But they can not tell him exactly *when* these things happened. *When* were the egg-shaped graves dug? In what year, or at least in what century, did the Old Ones start to build Cliff Palace? When did they leave it?

Archeologists wished for accurate dates in the Southwest, but for a long time they had no idea how to get them. Their only clue at first was something they *did not* find. Not a single horse bone, or cow bone, ever turned up in the Old Ones' garbage heaps. Horses and cattle did not come to the Southwest until the Spaniards brought them in the year 1540. It seemed clear that the Old Ones had moved away from their homes before horses and cattle arrived — that is, before 1540.

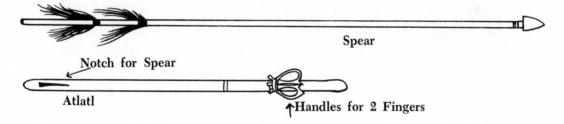

Spear

Notch for Spear

Atlatl

↑Handles for 2 Fingers

Before bows and arrows came to the Southwest, men used spears which they hurled with the help of a spear thrower, sometimes called an atlatl. Archeologists easily recognized spear throwers because Eskimos and some other peoples still use them.

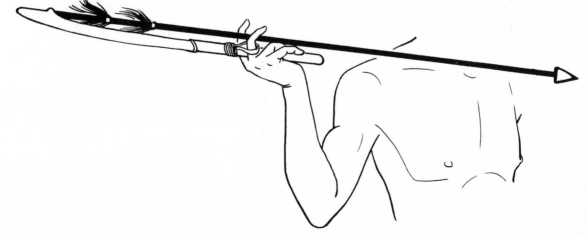

This was as close to a definite date as archeologists could come — until they found that calendars had actually been growing all around them in the trunks of pine and fir trees.

Calendars in Trees

Every year a living tree gets thicker. A layer of new wood grows in between the bark and the old layer that grew last year. In some trees such as pine and fir, each layer shows up very clearly. If you examine a tree stump or the end of a log, the layers look like separate rings or bands in the wood. Count them and you can tell how old the tree was when it died. The ring at the center shows the first year of growth. The outside ring shows the last year.

Look at the rings carefully and you can also see that some are wider than others. That means the tree grew more in some years than in others. Why? Because the weather was different in different years.

If one tree grows a lot in any particular year, all the others in that part of the world will grow a lot, too. All of them will add a wide ring of new wood.

The story of how this information turned into a tree-calendar begins with a scientist named A. E. Douglass whose main interest was stars, not ruins or even trees. Douglass wanted to find out all he could

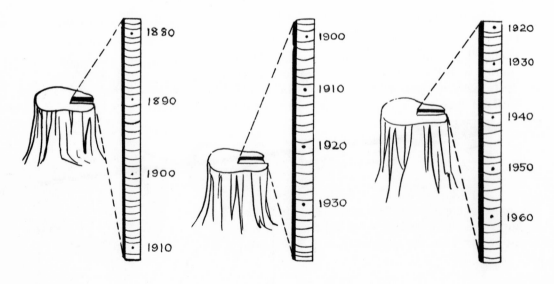

about certain mysterious spots that appeared on the sun every ten or eleven years. In particular, he wanted to know if these spots had any effect on the weather here on earth. Of course he looked at weather reports, but he could not get enough of them to prove anything. Nobody kept accurate weather records until quite recently. Douglass needed information that went back hundreds of years.

One day an exciting idea came to him. The record he wanted could be found in the growth rings of pine and fir trees. The older the trees, the longer the record would be. This meant he needed samples of very old wood.

Where could he find ancient wood? In ancient ruins, of course. Archeologists digging in the ruins were glad to cooperate. They gave Douglass the samples he needed. In return he gave the archeologists a rich reward. He told them the age of the ruins they were excavating.

Trees Answer Questions

To make his tree-ring calendar, Douglass studied the wide rings and narrow rings on many Southwestern trees. Then he made up a growth chart. The chart showed how there were wide rings, narrow rings, all sizes of rings in young living trees, then in older trees, and still older trees. The picture on page 34 shows how wood from three trees makes a calendar that goes back more than 80 years.

Gradually, Douglass and the archeologists put together a tree ring chart that goes back 2000 years. Now it is easy to tell the age of any ruined building in the Southwest, provided that you can get a sample of wood, or even charcoal, from one of its beams. You can make a chart of the rings in the sample. Then you compare this chart with the big

An archeologist found this object made of corn husks in a cliff dwelling. What did the Old Ones use it for? Turn the page and you will find out.

chart that covers 2000 years. When you find a section of the big chart where the pattern of wide and narrow rings matches the pattern in your small chart, you have succeeded. Dates on the big chart tell the exact year when a stone axe cut down the tree from which your sample came. That is pretty sure to be the year when the house itself was built.

It is fun to know just how old an ancient house is, and archeologists like to solve the mysteries of time. But a date all by itself is not very important. A scientist wants to know much more than dates. When he first looks at a lot of ancient ruined villages, it is as if he were looking at a book that has been torn apart. But if he can put the pages together correctly, he can read a story — a story with a beginning, a middle and an end. Dates are like page numbers. Using dates, the archeologists have figured out how the chapters followed each other in the story of the Old Ones.

Because an astronomer and some archeologists worked together, we can answer questions that puzzled even the experts for a long time after Richard Wetherill discovered Cliff Palace in Mesa Verde.

How old is Cliff Palace? Tree rings tell us that people started building homes there in the year 1073. They kept on building new ones for exactly two hundred years. The newest beam in Cliff Palace came from a tree that was cut down in the year 1273.

The doughnut-shaped object on page 35 is a pad which a woman put on her head when she was carrying a jar of water.

Why did the Old Ones stop building in Cliff Palace? Why did they leave the homes of their ancestors? Can tree rings answer these questions, too?

The rings in the trees of the Southwest are very thin for all the years from 1276 to 1299. Trees grew very, very little for twenty-three years. It seems as if the weather was wrong for the growth of trees. Perhaps the weather was also wrong for the growth of corn and beans and squash. Maybe the Old Ones who lived in Cliff Palace moved away in search of food or water.

This sounds possible. But take a good second look at the tree ring dates. The latest beam in Cliff Palace was cut three years *before* the long stretch of bad weather arrived. Maybe the Old Ones had already moved away by the time bad weather arrived.

Tree rings in many ruined villages show that people had stopped building new homes before the slow-growth years. That was true of the biggest town of all—Pueblo Bonito. Its houses had been abandoned *long* before people left Cliff Palace. Why?

Perhaps we can find a clue in the houses themselves.

Walls Without Doors

Houses tell a great many things about the people who build and live in them. Of course, a house shows what materials its builder knew how to use, what tools he had borrowed or invented. Houses can tell whether people are divided into rich and poor, owners and slaves. They can even tell us whether people are happy and carefree or worried and full of fear.

Look at the picture of Pueblo Bonito, the Beautiful Town where more than a thousand people once lived. Do you see anything odd about it? The whole outside wall is blank. There is not a single gate or door. However, if you could look at the ruin itself, you would see a few dim outlines of doorways. The openings were sealed up with strong masonry. Why? Why did people shut themselves in behind a wall? The most sensible answer seems to be that they were afraid.

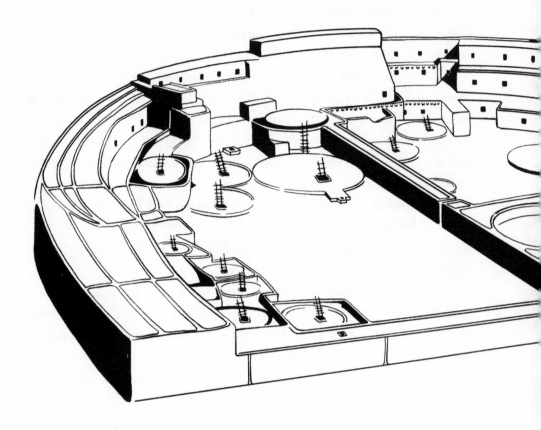

One kind of fear, even today, makes people build walls and close doors—fear of robbers. Pueblo Bonito was filled with things that robbers might be tempted to steal. Its jewelers made lovely turquoise beads. Its storerooms held plenty of corn that the men raised in fields near the town. Did people in neighboring villages become jealous of all this wealth and try to steal it? Such a thing has happened often in the world, but archeologists have found very little evidence that the Old Ones raided each other. They were peaceful farmers.

However, there *is* evidence that strangers began to wander into the Southwest. They were hunters, not farmers. They did not know how to raise corn, although they quickly learned to like it after they captured some women who showed them how to cook it. When game was

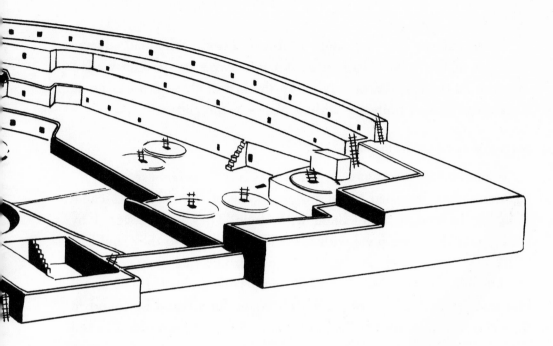

This is a model showing what Pueblo Bonito must have looked like after its people sealed up all outside doors and gateways for fear of raiders.

scarce — and it was often very scarce — the hungry wanderers thought about the food stored up in Pueblo Bonito. They could see the beauty and value of turquoise, too. So they attacked the peaceful farmers again and again.

At Pueblo Bonito people tried to protect themselves by blocking the doors. To get in and out of town they climbed ladders which could be pulled up onto the roof for safety. But the robbers could still ambush men at work in the fields. Or they could bring ladders of their own at night and climb the walls to make a raid.

Finally the farmers gave up the battle against the wandering hunters. They moved away — those who were still alive — and started over again in a new place, hoping that the raiders would not follow and discover them.

Other villages had the same problem. People who had always lived out in the open began to crowd into caves in the cliff-walled canyons. In the end the raiders drove the last of these farmers away from even the best protected hiding places in the cliffs.

Secret Rooms Underground

Where did the Old Ones go when they left their homes?

Many clues have led to an answer. Some of the best clues came from big, mysterious holes lined with stone. They were covered by strong roofs that were level with the earth all around so they could be walked on. When explorers first saw these curious pits, they could not imagine why the Old Ones had built them. Then archeologists learned that underground rooms of exactly the same kind could be found in the villages of present-day Pueblo Indians. Some of the Indians called a room like this a kiva (KEY-vah), and the men used it for secret club meetings and religious ceremonies. Between ceremonies, such things as prayer sticks were kept in the kivas. Could it be that the strange big holes in the ancient ruins had been used in the same way? Sure enough, the ancient underground rooms contained prayer sticks and other ceremonial things.

Pueblo Indian men sometimes do weaving in their kivas. Did the Old Ones have this custom? Yes, they did. In the floors of ancient underground rooms archeologists found built-in loom anchors— gadgets that held looms steady while weavers worked.

Could it be that modern Pueblo Indians got the idea of kivas from the Old Ones? Were the Pueblos themselves descended from the Old Ones? After archeologists had studied evidence of all kinds, they felt sure that the answer to both questions was "yes!"

The mystery that puzzled Richard Wetherill when he discovered Cliff Palace has been solved. The Old Ones did not vanish. Not all of them were killed by robbers. Not every one died when the crops failed. Some at least managed to escape from enemies or famine. They moved into other towns in the Southwest where the people welcomed reinforcements. So the descendants of the Old Ones still live not far from the villages they abandoned so long ago.

Archeologists have dug into hundreds of villages in the Southwest. They have gathered bushels of facts, and they have learned a very great deal about the ancient people who left only *things* for us to wonder about. At the same time our scientific detectives have learned much about archeology itself. The fact is, archeology was just getting started in the Americas when Richard Wetherill was digging mummies from the floors of caves. Since then, men and women have kept on inventing tools and thinking up ideas to use in detective work all over the Americas.

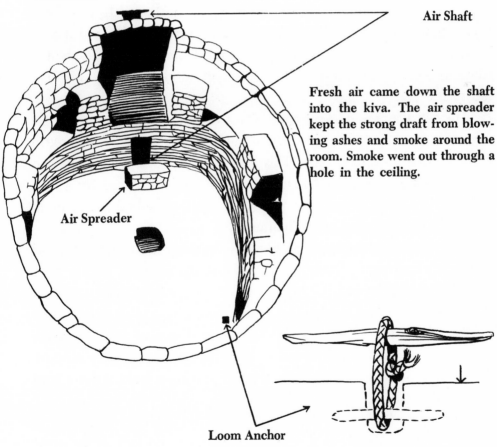

Air Shaft

Fresh air came down the shaft into the kiva. The air spreader kept the strong draft from blowing ashes and smoke around the room. Smoke went out through a hole in the ceiling.

Air Spreader

Loom Anchor

3

Lost Cities in the Jungle

On a certain day more than two hundred and fifty years ago, a man in tattered clothes stumbled through the jungle in Guatemala. Suddenly he stopped and stared almost straight up through an opening in the tree tops as if he saw a vision.

High in the sunlight glistened a huge building!

The man was Father Avendano, a Spanish missionary, who had been lost in the jungle for a month. His food was all gone and he felt weak and ill from hunger. This tall building, he thought, must be a dream that came to him because he had a fever. But it would not go away as dreams do. Soon his curiosity forced him toward the shining thing in the sky. Somehow he found energy to climb up the hill that led to it.

The hill was steep. Avendano clung to the weird roots of jungle trees that stuck out everywhere. He pushed aside vines that hung in his way, like great cobwebs. This was painful work. The vines had thorns as sharp as knives. The climb would have been hard for a man who was well and strong, but Avendano finally reached the summit, and there he marvelled more than ever.

The stone building was real, bigger even than he had thought, and strangest of all, more buildings like it rose up near by, higher than the tallest jungle trees.

Avendano looked inside. The rooms were tiny and deserted. Only monkeys lived here, no people. What did it all mean? He wondered, but he was too sick and starved to hunt for an answer. It was more important now to scramble down the hill and keep looking for a trail that would lead out of the jungle.

More dead than alive the priest finally did reach civilization. As matters turned out, he never came back for a second look at the great

buildings he was the first European to see, but he wrote a description of them. For a long time no one seemed to care about the strange ruins in the center of an uninhabited jungle. No one, including Father Avendano, dreamed that he had stumbled on the remains of a great city where thousands of people once attended religious ceremonies.

The weary missionary had no idea that he stood in a place where priests of another religion had worshipped, before Christianity reached his native Spain. These same pagan priests studied astronomy and wrote books filled with prophecies and rules for ceremonies and exact information about the sun and moon and stars. In fact they were so careful that they worked out a calendar as accurate as the one Avendano himself used. Yet all these marvels had been completely lost to the world.

The ghost city remained almost unknown for a hundred and fifty years. So did others that Avendano missed seeing. Then explorers began to visit the jungles. Later, archeologists made their way along dim trails that had been cut like tunnels through the tropical forests. The reason for these trails was something you would never guess— chewing gum.

Chewing gum is made from a thick juice called chicle which flows out of cuts in the bark of the sapodilla tree. When gum factories began to buy chicle, men went into the jungle looking for sapodilla trees. In a number of places they came across great ruined temples and half-buried stones with strange figures carved on them.

These chicle gatherers worked only in the rainy season when sap oozed from the trees. During the dry season they and their mules could take scientists into the heavy, quiet forests to the many ruins where no one lived any more.

Avendano's ghost city, which was now called Tikal (tee-KAHL), at last had visitors eager to solve its mysteries. But digging was impossible in the rainy season. When the rain stopped, water holes soon dried up. Tikal's ancient reservoirs would have to be cleaned and mended before they could be used again. Tools and supplies and food for expeditions had to come by muleback over the difficult trails. One

Indians built shelters for scientists at Tikal. They made a frame of poles which they tied together with vines. Then they covered it with a roof of palm leaves. The farmers and workmen of ancient Tikal lived in just such houses around the city.

archeologist after another cleared the jungle away, dug for a while, and went home with very little accomplished.

Meantime the chewing-gum people had transportation problems, too. Partly in order to speed up the delivery of chicle, the government of Guatemala made airfields in the forests where the sapodilla trees grew. Finally, in 1955, an airstrip was built at Tikal itself. Scientists from the University of Pennsylvania set up a camp and started the digging they had dreamed about doing for a long time.

During several months of each year now, workmen with the help of modern machinery strip jungle growth off the ruined city, and archeologists patiently rebuild it. This work will take a long time, but when it is done, Tikal will be a great public park which anyone can visit.

The great city of Tikal in Guatemala looked like this more than a thousand years ago. The buildings on top of the tall pyramids were temples with carved and painted roofs of stone. There priests in gorgeous costumes with feathered headdresses held ceremonies while the people watched from the huge square below. Smaller buildings were home for the priests.

46

Ordinary people lived in huts in the suburbs or on farms farther away. They came in often for ceremonies, and every fifth day they held a market where they traded for salt, chocolate, beautiful feathers, sharp stone knives, cotton cloth, and many other things.

47

The Secret of the Well

How do we know what went on in ancient Tikal?

To begin with, Tikal is only one of many cities left by the ancient Maya (MAH-yuh) Indians of Central America. The Mayas built temples by the dozen, and their artists decorated some of the walls with paintings which they crammed full of fascinating details about Mayan life. Somehow, by unbelievable good luck, a few of these paintings have lasted for hundreds of years, in spite of jungle heat and dampness.

Also the Mayas used to set up tall, stone pillars covered with endless carvings and decorations which are so complicated that it makes you dizzy to look at them. Some of the carvings show gods in the form of strange, made-up animals. Others are portraits of real people—rulers, priests, and soldiers.

Some facts about the Mayas—not very many—can be found in books written by Spaniards who invaded Maya land. But most of our knowledge comes from exploration in the ruins themselves. Much has been discovered at a magnificent place called Chichen Itza (chee-CHAIN eet-SAH). Several famous archeologists have dug there. One

Archeologists study all kinds of things from ancient graves in order to find out what Indian life was long ago.

was Edward Herbert Thompson, who made a sensational discovery because he believed an old story about a well, a story that everybody else thought was only a fable.

This well was sacred to Mayan gods. It was very wide and very deep, but people did not take water from it. Instead, the priests used it as a place for religious sacrifices. The Mayas believed that if the gods got angry they would hold back rain, and this of course would spoil the corn crops. Valuable gifts were supposed to prevent or cure the gods' anger, and the priests threw all kinds of precious objects into the sacred well. They tossed in pottery, jewels, golden ornaments. If that did not seem to be enough, they sacrificed human beings, the most valuable offering. Prisoners of war and beautiful young girls were thrown over the edge to be swallowed by the water far below.

This small pottery statue of a Mayan god is hollow. The mouth is a chimney which lets out smoke when incense burns inside. The legs of the stool are made of human bones.

So went the story that Thompson read in an old Spanish book. When he visited Chichen Itza, he found things that exactly fitted the description in the book. The well itself was really a sunken pond nearly two hundred feet across. A perpendicular wall of rock surrounded it. At one place where this cliff wall dropped away from the flat surface of the land, a platform had been built. Standing there on the brink, priests could fling their sacrifices into the well.

The water below was deep—eighty feet deep. In the mud at the bottom lay the ancient things that Thompson wanted to find. But how could anybody get at them? Was it possible to dig up treasure hidden for centuries at the bottom of a very big, very deep well?

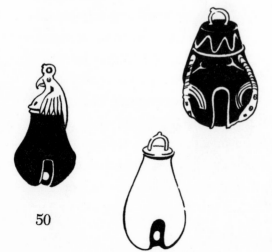

Mayan pictures often show the god of death wearing bells. Perhaps that explains why so many gold bells like these were found in the Sacred Well.

50

Archeologists often reconstruct ruined buildings. Here workmen are moving a beam of very heavy zapote wood that will be used over a doorway in the Temple of the Giant Jaguar at Tikal.

Most people would have answered, "No." But Thompson was enthusiastic about trying. He managed to bring in dredging equipment and rigged it up at the top of the cliff. Four men turning a crank lowered the dredge till its jaws touched bottom and took a bite out of the mud. Then they cranked the load up and dumped it on dry land.

The first bite held nothing of value. This did not surprise Thompson. The next load and the next and the next showed no sign of anything that the Mayan priests might have flung into the water. Up and down, day after day, the men cranked and Thompson searched the muck that the dredge produced. Still, not one sign of treasure appeared.

51

The picture on this vase shows a priest. Some Mayan priests covered themselves with black pigment or black cloth. This man's forehead slopes because his mother bound his head to a board when he was a baby.

Then one day he spied some strange little balls in the mud. These proved to be the kind of resin that Mayan priests burned at ceremonies. More resin balls. The priests had at least thrown incense into the well.

Another bite from the bottom—another and another—and finally the dredge brought up the reward for Thompson's patience. Out of the muck came gold ornaments, beautifully decorated plates and vases, fancy spear points, bowls carved from lovely green stone, little golden bells — and the skeletons of girls and men.

52

Thompson proved that the story in the old Spanish book was true. More important, the *things* he found told archeologists a great deal about the Mayan *people*.

A Hunch Pays Off

Later, in the same big Mayan city of Chichen Itza, another archeologist decided to try out a hunch he had. This man was the same Earl Morris who had done a lot of digging in the ruins left by the Old Ones in southwestern United States. Morris got his idea one day when he was idly comparing the Old Ones and the Mayans. There were differences, of course, but he had noticed many similarities, too.

He remembered the little collections of precious shells and turquoise that he found buried in ancient kivas. These, he supposed, were religious offerings the Old Ones made at the time they built the kivas. Was it possible that the Mayas, too, made such offerings? Nobody had ever found any, but the longer Morris thought about it, the stronger his hunch became that Mayan temples might contain hidden gifts to the gods.

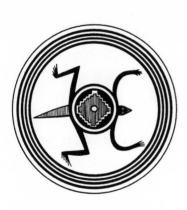 

People often broke holes in the pots that they buried with the dead. This "killed" the pot, so that its spirit could make the long journey to the next world. The "killed" dish on the right was found in a Mayan grave, the one on the left came from a grave in New Mexico.

At Chichen Itza, Morris had taken on the job of uncovering and rebuilding a huge place called the Temple of the Warriors. It turned out to be two temples, one completely buried under the other. When the work on both was all done, Morris decided to have some extra fun. He would test his hunch. He would look for a buried offering.

Where would the Mayas have hidden a secret gift to the gods? Probably in the most sacred place—that is—in or near an altar. There were several altars to choose from in the Temple of the Warriors. At the first altar, Morris discovered that some red plaster had been gouged away and then replaced with a white patch. He dug in and found a pot, but it was broken and empty. Thieves must have got there first. Perhaps the robbers were scared away before they could paint the new plaster red to finish concealing their crime. At any rate, *there had been something hidden in the altar.*

Excitedly, Morris continued the search. He found that the other two altars also had secret holes, but for one reason or another nothing much remained in them. That finished the outer temple. Now for a search in the older one that had been buried underneath it.

Morris began to examine the floor of the old temple where the altar once stood. With a pick he tapped on one stone slab after another. The sound was the same everywhere — except possibly at one spot. Here he whacked again, and the pick broke through into a cavity.

Beneath the floor sat a stone jar. From it Morris took a wonderfully polished round ball of jade. Mayan priests had used the ball to foretell the future, the way crystal gazers tell fortunes today. Next to the ball lay beads and ornaments. And at the bottom of the stone container was something that looked like a beautiful blue plate. It was made from 3,000 tiny pieces of turquoise that had been cemented together in a design unlike anything found in Mayan temples before.

Morris's hunch, based on great knowledge of the ways of Indians, had led to a marvelous find.

54

The Temple of the Warriors looked like this after archeologist Earl Morris dug it out from under a mound covered with brush and trees.

Man-Made Mountains

The small temple that Morris discovered underneath the Temple of the Warriors was not the only one of its kind in Maya land. Archeologists have found such places over and over again. The custom of burying whole buildings is strange enough, but think of this: The hills on which these ancient temples stand are made-made. Human beings piled up the huge mounds by hand. Men, women, and children carried, pushed, lifted, dragged tons and tons of earth and stone without any machinery or wagons or carts or wheelbarrows, or even any animals to help them pull.

When one of the artificial hills was finished it looked like a pyramid, which was made of giant-sized stairs and chopped off at the top. The sides of the pyramid were then given a thick coat of plaster or stucco. Finally, architects and masons built a temple on the flat top, using blocks of limestone carefully cut and shaped.

If you think that all this work took a tremendous amount of time, you are right. Every year thousands of Mayas put in many weeks of

The Mayas placed big stone pillars near their temples. A god is carved on the front of this one. The markings carved on the side show a date that was important in the Mayan religious calendar. Descendants of the Maya still burn incense in front of some of the pillars near ancient ruined temples.

labor on construction projects. They spent a great deal of time attending religious ceremonies too. Obviously, when they were doing these things, they were not growing food for themselves. How then did Mayas solve the food problem?

Corn solved it for them. A man could feed his entire family for a whole year with less than three months of work in a good cornfield. If he worked more days and planted more than he needed, he could help feed the priests and other city dwellers. If seeds were planted at the right time, crops grew so easily in the tropical climate that people had a great deal of time to spare. Led by their priests they spent an immense amount of time on religion. Since they had many gods they put up many temples. They made fine, wide roads for pilgrims to walk on when they journeyed to the cities. They built houses for the priests and nobles and huge stone-walled courts where they played a kind of basketball as part of religious ceremonies.

For some strange reason the Mayas would use a city for a while, and then would move away and let it go to ruin. One after another, their magnificent buildings were abandoned. Tikal, once the home of a great many people, disappeared under a growth of jungle trees and vines. Why?

Archeologists are still hunting for an answer to the question. Some believe that it happened like this: In the beginning, farmers clustered around the outskirts of a city. Each family cleared a field by burning down trees and brush. Year after year crops were planted in the same fields, and year after year the crops got smaller. The Mayas had not discovered that soil needs fertilizer, but they did know that plants grew well on land that was newly cleared. When the old soil wore out near the city, farmers made new fields farther away and started wearing out the soil all over again. This went on until the farms were so far from the temple city that priests ordered the building of new temples nearer the farms.

Some archeologists think there may have been another reason why cities fell to ruin: The common people got tired of doing such tremendous amounts of work. They overthrew the priests and abandoned the temples. Jungle then moved in on the great, empty, stone buildings.

Certainly the common people had the job of providing priests with all necessities and luxuries. They worked very hard carrying out the priests' orders. Maybe they did get to talking among themselves and decided that all this was not worthwhile. The ruler of one Mayan city

If you found a big heavy round stone like this near a ruined Mayan temple, would you know what it was? Turn the page and see.

57

told the Spaniards that he always gave his people a great deal of work to do so that they would not have time to plot rebellion against him.

This idea may explain a good deal in Mayan life. For instance, it could be the reason why priests had new temples built on top of perfectly good temples that were already there.

Whatever happened, this much is true: The Mayan religion was very complicated, and the priests were not only powerful rulers, they were very learned in their own special way. They spent great energy keeping track of the days and the months and the years. In the begin-

A Mayan Basketball Hoop—Players had to knock a hard rubber ball through the hoop, using only elbows, knees, and feet—never hands.

ning, there was a reason for this. It is necessary to plant corn in Maya land at just the right time in order to get full benefit of the rainy season. The priests studied the sun and the stars, and they learned to predict when the rainy season was likely to start each year. From that discovery they went on and figured out a calendar. The idea of time grew more and more important to them. They kept careful track of the years and made a special point of counting them by twenties. It became part of the Mayan religion to set up carved stone markers at the end of each twenty-year period. In some places markers were set up every ten years and even every five years.

Mayas went to a great deal of trouble to mark off the passing of the years. They actually worshipped time.

Breaking the Code

The picture on page 56 shows one of the Mayan time markers. You would not guess that the carvings on it were dates. There is nothing here that looks like any number or word you ever saw. Archeologists could not understand the carvings either when they first stumbled on these strange-looking stones in the jungle.

Gradually, the experts found out the meaning of many of the designs on the stones. These designs are called glyphs (GLIFFS). Each glyph is a drawing that stands for a number or a word or a part of a word. (The Chinese use this same method of making designs stand for whole words.)

Archeologists have cracked the Mayan number code. They can read Mayan dates and can tell you the exact order in which the pillars were set up. They know that Tikal was one of the early Mayan cities, and that Chichen Itza was one of the last. There is no longer any secret about how long people lived in and around their cities.

The highest Mayan number that archeologists have yet found. In our figures it reads 400,000,000 years.

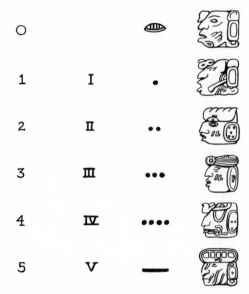

We can write figures in two different ways. So could the Mayas. Sometimes they used dots and bars; sometimes they used "Head" numerals. There were nineteen different "Head" numerals, plus zero.

Experts agree on these things, but they do not agree on another very important matter. They can not tell us exactly *when*, according to our calendar, any event in Mayan history took place. One theory puts everything in Mayan history 260 years earlier than another theory. Soon archeologists will probably learn which is correct.

What the Skin Divers Found

The land of the Mayas is still as rich in surprises as it was when Father Avendano stumbled on the shining temple at Tikal. In 1955 a skin diver in Guatemala went down into the warm waters of Lake Amatitlan (AH-mah-teet-LAHN) to look for good fishing holes. He came up with ancient Mayan jars.

He and his friends were fascinated and made more dives. Altogether they brought up five hundred jars, figurines, and incense burners. This collection gave archeologists a lot of new puzzles to solve.

Why were many of the bowls found in neat piles? Even more puzzling, what were incense burners doing underwater where they could not possibly burn?

Scientists have not finished studying Lake Amatitlan, but they have made some guesses about it. Perhaps people came here, as they did to the Sacred Well at Chichen Itza, and made offerings to the gods. Certainly it is a strange and special place. Along the shore, geysers like those in Yellowstone Park sometimes shoot into the air. There are springs of water so hot that you could hardboil an egg in them. A live volcano stands near by. It has shot off several times in the last five hundred years. At a place where there are such goings-on, the level of the water in the lake might rise and fall, too. Maybe, when the lake was low, people set bowls and incense burners along the shore as offerings to the gods of this mysterious spot. Later when the lake rose, the bowls and burners stayed underwater.

Amatitlan still holds many secrets. So do other lakes and wells. Skin divers have gone down into one well at a place called Dzibilchaltun (JIBB-ill-chahl-TOON) only seventy-five miles from Chichen Itza. The treasure they have brought up so far does not include any gold, but it is valuable for another reason. It is helping archeologists to find out more about the city that once surrounded the well. This city was huge, and it seems to be among the first that the Mayas built.

But, archeologists are asking themselves, what is this particular city doing in this particular place? They had thought that only the youngest Mayan cities could be found in this neighborhood.

It begins to look as if many archeologists still have a great deal of detective work to do before we can understand the mystery of the Mayas who built so many cities so many years ago.

POP   UO   ZIP   ZOTZ

TZEC   XUL   YAXKIN   MOL

CHEN   YAX   ZAC   CEH

MAC   KANKIN   MUAN   PAX

KAYAB   CUMHU   UAYEB

This is the way the Mayas wrote the names of the 19 months of their year.

62

4

Wells, Bells and Ball Games

There was a curious thing about the treasure that Edward Herbert Thompson dredged up from the Sacred Well at the city of Chichen Itza. Very few of the gold and copper objects he found there had been made in the city itself. Indeed, most of them did not come from *any* part of Maya land.

How do we know this? First of all, we can search high and low in some of the ruins, and we shall find no gold at all. In others there is very little. Mayan craftsmen did not do much work with gold or any other metal, and it is easy to recognize what they did make. Their work has a distinct Mayan style. Craftsmen in other places had their own styles, too, and an experienced person can usually tell at a glance where an ornament or bell or plate was made.

However, an archeologist does not like to judge things simply by the way they look. Whenever he can, he checks his opinions with scientific tests. It happens that the metals used by craftsmen in Central America made checking easy. In each area the metals had their own distinct impurities. To find the source of a trinket from the Sacred Well, a chemist checks the impurities in the metal.

There is also an electrical machine that tests metal. This machine uses tiny specks of gold that can be taken from small precious objects, without leaving a noticeable mark. By testing and by studying different styles of work, experts have learned that many things in the Sacred Well came from Costa Rica, Panama, and Honduras. Other things came from the Valley of Mexico, several hundred miles in the opposite direction. A few were shaped in another style that the experts felt sure they recognized. These pieces must have travelled by canoe or jungle trail from Colombia in South America. This seemed impos-

63

sible. Nevertheless, the tests showed that the golden trinkets had, indeed, been made in Colombia more than 1400 miles away.

What did all this mean? For one thing, it proved that some people in ancient Central America moved around a great deal. The gold did not get from one place to another all by itself. Traders no doubt carried part of it. Perhaps, stay-at-homes in Chichen Itza bought gold ornaments from a travelling merchant and, later, sacrificed them in the Well. Religious pilgrims must have brought many things with them. Perhaps, some pilgrims came all the way from the very towns where gold objects were manufactured.

Archeologists have found many interesting gold ornaments in graves in Panama, but very often robbers have beaten them to the treasure. The greatest robbers of all were the Spaniards who conquered Central America. They seized every bit of gold they could find, and they found a great deal. From the funeral of one Panama chief who had just died, they took 355 pounds of it, all carefully worked into curious, intricate shapes.

The Spaniards did not care a hoot about the objects themselves. They were not archeologists trying to learn about the achievements of people different from themselves. Greed pure and simple drove them to look for treasure. They melted down whatever they laid hands on and made the gold into bars that could be weighed and used for money. Fortunately, there were some things they missed.

The Rubber People

Close to Maya land, on the east coast of Mexico, explorers once found some very startling objects: great, round, carved stone heads that looked like baby-faced football players wearing helmets. Archeologists tell us that these strange carvings were made by people they call Olmecs (OHL-mecks).

Olmec means Rubber People, and a legend says it was they who discovered how to make rubber from the sap of a certain jungle tree. Possibly, Olmecs also invented rubber balls and the kind of basket-

How an Ancient Jade Carver Worked

First the craftsman sawed off a piece of jade in the general shape he wanted. His saw was a string. The teeth of the saw were nothing but bits of moist sand. By rubbing the string back and forth he made the sand bite into the tough jade.

With a stone hammer he began to peck out the features.

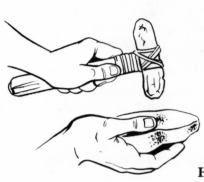

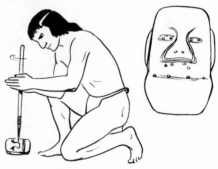

He made deeper cuts with a drill and moist sand. His drill was either a hollow reed or a sheet of copper rolled to form a tube and attached to a stick. By whirling the drill back and forth with the palms of his hands, he made the sand cut circles into the jade.

For shallow gouging and scraping, he used a tool like this.

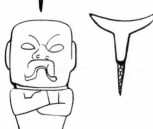

The final smoothing was probably done with sand, but no one knows exactly how a stone carver gave jade its beautiful polish.

65

The Olmecs carved many huge baby-faced heads like this. One of them weighs ten tons. Ancient engineers moved it ten miles from the quarry, over swampy land and across a deep ravine.

ball game that was once popular all the way from Guatemala to Arizona.

The first archeologists' report on this game was published in 1891, the year in which modern basketball was invented. Perhaps the inventor got part of his idea for our popular sport from ancient Indians.

No one knows whether the Olmecs were really the first basketball players, and this is only one in a long list of unsolved mysteries about them. Why did they carve the enormous, stone heads that all resembled each other? Were these the images of a baby-faced god?

Why did one of these huge heads have a hole bored through it from the ear to the mouth? Did some sly priest use it to fool people? Did he talk secretly into the ear, then claim that the god's voice came out of the mouth?

Apparently the Olmecs lived a very long time ago, yet they had a system of writing with glyphs that resembled Mayan glyphs. Were the Olmecs older than the Mayas? Did Olmecs invent writing and teach it to the Mayas?

66

The postage stamp gives an idea of the size of this duck-billed god which an Olmec artist carved from jade.

It is easier to ask these questions than to answer them. Sometimes an expert thinks he has found an answer when he has only added other questions. Look at the funny little statue of a duck-billed god, for instance. The squiggles scratched on it tell a date. If we believe what the date says, then the statue is about two thousand years old. But there is another possibility. Perhaps the Olmec sculptor carved it in honor of a past event—the way a sculptor today might carve the date 1620 on a statue of the Pilgrims landing at Plymouth.

Scholars have not yet agreed about the age of the Olmecs, but one thing seems certain: These lively, imaginative people had ideas that spread to other parts of Mexico.

Fabulous Mountain

In southern Mexico there is a fascinating mountain called Monte Alban (MOHN-tay al-BAHN). Long ago, ancient people levelled off the top of it and began to build there. They kept on building for more

Olmecs and other Central Americans carved U-shaped stone objects. What for? Possibly the stones were imitations of wicker stomach pads, which basketball players wore in games. They must have worn the clumsy stone pads for religious ceremonies only.

than two thousand years, putting up temples, pyramids, platforms, tombs. At different times they had very different ways of doing things, and this makes the mountain especially tempting to an archeologist. It is like a many-decker sandwich with different fillings between the decks. When an archeologist bites down through it, he finds that each filling is distinct. It has its own taste and style. And, of course, this many-decker archeological sandwich has its oldest layer on the bottom.

The sandwich fillings at Monte Alban include jewelry, stone carvings, pottery, tools, and many other things. In the beginning, the people here made carvings of baby-faced gods the way the Olmecs did. Next, the craftsmen and builders followed Mayan styles. After that, a tribe of people called Zapotecs (sah-poh-TECKS) controlled Monte Alban, and they set a different fashion. They had a system of writing, but it seems unlike Mayan writing, and no one has yet figured out what it says. Then an enemy people called the Mixtecs (MISH-tecks) took Monte Alban away from the Zapotecs. The Mixtecs had many skilled goldsmiths who worked in still another style. Finally they were conquered by the warlike Aztecs.

The Mexican archeologist Alfonso Caso has done a great deal of digging at Monte Alban and has discovered many of its secrets, but one of his finds was in a class by itself.

In 1931 Caso and his helpers began digging down into some tombs that were buried in small mounds. The first few tombs had been robbed. Caso made a hole in the covering of another tomb and flashed a light into the cavity below. A skull, and beside it two vases, told him

68

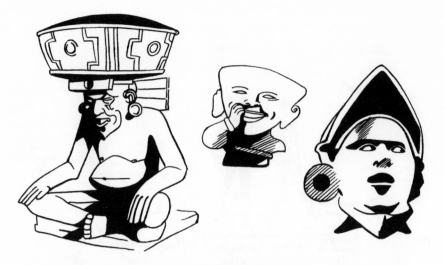

These figures were made by the Totonacs who lived near the Olmecs.

grave robbers had missed this place. One of his students, who was small and slender, wriggled through the opening and let out an astonished yell. Caso could not wait to make the hole larger. Somehow he managed to squeeze his big frame through.

The beam of his flashlight fell on a large marble vessel, a heap of bones, bells and beads of gold, golden bracelets — ten of them — and more bracelets made of silver. Near by lay a crown of gold with a golden feather. The wonders were just beginning.

The skull Caso had seen from above was inlaid all over with tiny bits of turquoise, and it did not belong to any of the bodies buried in the tomb. Instead, it seemed to be a kind of sacred object, a gift to the dead.

In Western Mexico people called Taras-cans made little figures like this.

69

Pearls and golden beads lay all over the floor. The two men did not dare move for fear they would destroy some treasure or disturb a clue that might help solve an ancient mystery. The careful way to enter and study this tomb would be from a tunnel at one end.

Although it was six o'clock at night, Caso's helpers started tunnelling. By three in the morning they reached the tomb. Methodically now—in the bright, hot light of a gasoline lamp—Caso measured and noted down the exact position of every object before he moved it. By dawn, he had taken out only thirty-five pieces.

With very little rest Caso and his crew labored on for a week, digging, sifting, sorting, describing the big things, the little things, the strange things they found. The number seemed endless. Altogether, more than 500 objects came from this one tomb—and Caso counted as a single "object" a necklace that had several hundred gold and pearl and turquoise beads. There were several such necklaces.

70

Mixtecs had left this treasure, but the tomb itself was originally built and used by Zapotecs. Why did the rich and powerful Mixtecs use a second-hand tomb for a first-rate burial?

Why? People have spent years looking for answers to questions like this. Curiosity drives men on to learn who did what, and when, and where things came from. Seeking has brought many answers. But Monte Alban is vast. It will be a long, long time before it gives up the complete story that it holds.

Master Builders

The treasure in the Sacred Well at Chichen Itza proved that people carried *things* great distances in ancient Central America.

Ideas also travelled. How can we be sure of this? For an answer look at the pictures. They show that ideas about building travelled to Chichen Itza from the city of Tula (TOO-lah), a thousand miles away in the Valley of Mexico. The people of Tula, who are now called

On the left, a Feathered Serpent pillar in the Toltec city of Tula. Right, Feathered Serpent pillars made much later at far-off Chichen Itza.

Toltecs (TOHL-tecks), used pillars to hold up the roofs of buildings. A Toltec pillar was often carved in the form of a snake with its tail up in the air and its head on the ground. This snake had feathers, and it represented a god known as the Feathered Serpent who encouraged art and learning.

An earlier people were also skillful builders. They created a great, well-planned religious center at Teotihuacan (TAY-oh-TEE-wah-KAHN). This City of Gods spread over an area two miles wide and three and a half miles long. Every inch of ground that was not covered by pyramids and temples was paved, then re-paved and paved again with hard white plaster. At least once, the priests had every temple in the place buried and another temple built on top of it. The amount of work the people did here was unbelievable, and the biggest labor of all was the Pyramid of the Sun.

Most pyramids consist of loose dirt and rock piled up and then covered with stone and plaster. The builders did cover the Pyramid of the Sun with stone and plaster, but first they went to the enormous, extra trouble of forming much of this pyramid out of bricks. They made each brick — individually — out of earth mixed with water, then dried it in the sun.

Why such vast labor?

This puzzle was enough to intrigue archeologists, but the bricks produced another puzzle just as fascinating. The material in them came, it seems, from a garbage dump. Who left this refuse heap which was obviously older than Teotihuacan?

What happened to the city itself in the end? Someone smashed its temples and knocked down the statues of gods. Who were the invaders that destroyed the city at a time when it was, perhaps, the greatest in all Mexico?

Archeologists keep looking for answers. The more they dig, the more they realize that Mexico and Central America have a very long history, and that people there created many centers of civilization.

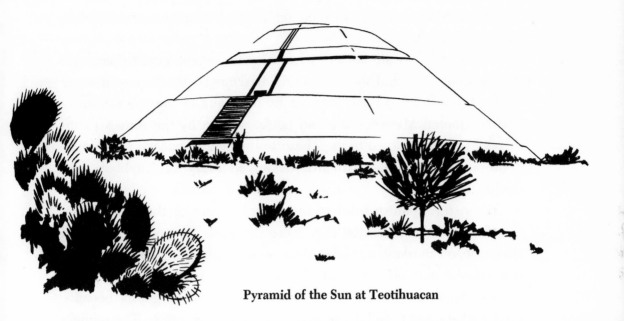

Pyramid of the Sun at Teotihuacan

Ruined People

The Aztecs are the most famous of all the ancient Indians in Mexico. Yet archeologists have dug up very few Aztec ruins. The truth is that they can not do much digging. The place where most of the Aztecs lived is now covered by Mexico City. You would have to tear down the home of the President of Mexico in order to find the remains of palaces that once belonged to Aztec rulers. Hotels and apartment houses stand where Aztec dwellings used to be. Stores and office buildings rise where jewellers and wood carvers worked and merchants traded feathers or cloth for cocoa beans.

Under the busy modern city lies a great deal of ancient material. This could tell archeologists much they want to know about the once powerful Aztecs. Glimpses of the buried past appear now and then when workmen dig a basement for a new building or shovel out a trench for sewer pipes. As a matter of fact, the Aztecs left an unusual amount of rubbish because of a curious custom they had: they broke

73

and discarded everything in their homes and temples every fifty-two years.

Fortunately, we do not need to wait for archeologists to piece together what they find in ditches and basements. We can read some of the Aztec story in books written by members of the Spanish army that conquered Mexico. Fourteen books written by the Aztecs themselves have come down to us. These tell us much, but we shall never know all, because the Spaniards destroyed every Indian book they could find.

When the Spanish soldiers first caught sight of the great Aztec city, some of them thought they were dreaming. It stood, a splendid spectacle, on an island in a lake. Wide stone roads built above the water connected it with other magnificent cities on the shore.

The Spanish invaders were received as honored guests because their visit seemed to fulfill a prophecy made by the priests. The soldiers wandered around the city, and at every turn they found new wonders. There was a zoo full of brilliant feathered birds and strange animals, including a shaggy American buffalo brought from plains far to the north. This was the first buffalo that Europeans had ever seen; also it was the first zoo. There were none in Europe.

The soldiers found schools, too, where boys learned various trades. Astronomer-priests kept track of the stars and the calendar. Government officials knew how to do arithmetic and a kind of picture writing that was different from the glyphs used by the Mayas.

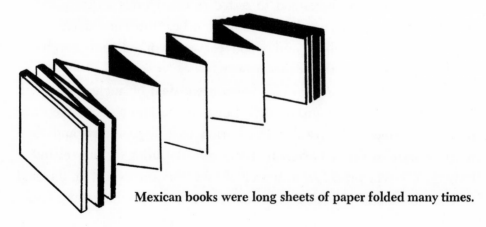

Mexican books were long sheets of paper folded many times.

74

The great Aztec temple in the center of Mexico City looked like this when the Spaniards first saw it in the year 1519. To go from place to place in the city, people often paddled dugout canoes along the many canals.

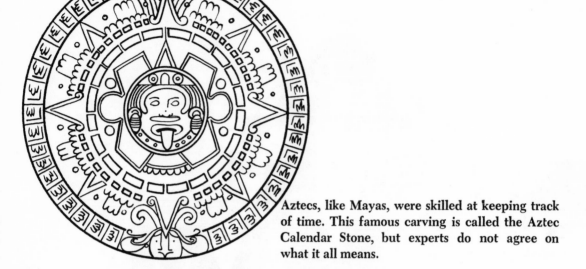

Aztecs, like Mayas, were skilled at keeping track of time. This famous carving is called the Aztec Calendar Stone, but experts do not agree on what it all means.

The Aztecs obviously needed a way to write. They had an enormous amount of bookkeeping to do because they collected large taxes from the many tribes they had conquered. The government used so much paper for record-keeping that certain towns had to pay their taxes in paper. One town alone sent 480,000 sheets a year to Mexico City.

The Aztecs fought wars to get wealth, but they fought for a religious reason too. They thought that the gods long ago gave some of their own blood to create human beings, and people ought to give human blood to the gods in return. The Sun God would die and leave the world in darkness if he did not receive blood from human beings. Believing this, the Aztecs fought wars to get captives whom they sacrificed to keep the sun alive and shining. It was supposed to be a privilege to die this way. A person who was sacrificed got the best possible reward: he went to one of the highest and most desirable of the thirteen Aztec heavens.

Many other peoples all over the world have practiced human sacrifice, but the Aztecs carried it to greater extremes. In fact, they did many things in a big way. They built tremendous roads from the

76

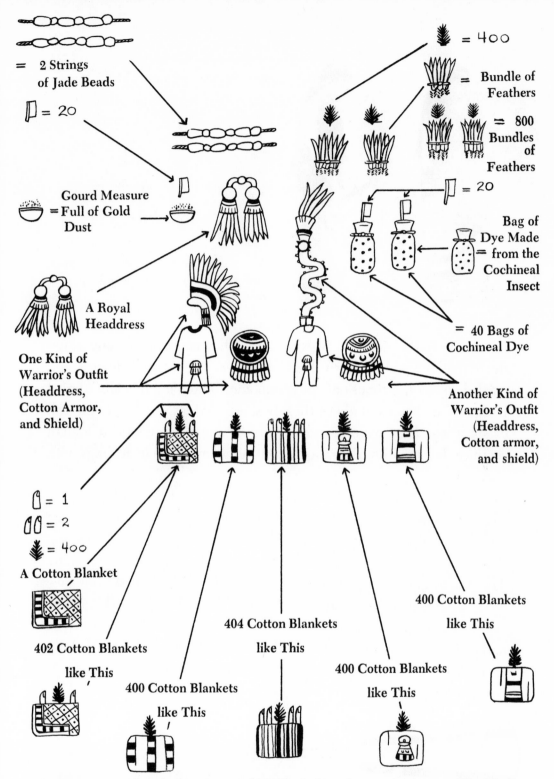

= 2 Strings of Jade Beads

= 20

Gourd Measure = Full of Gold Dust

A Royal Headdress

One Kind of Warrior's Outfit (Headdress, Cotton Armor, and Shield)

= 1

= 2

= 400

A Cotton Blanket

402 Cotton Blankets like This

400 Cotton Blankets like This

404 Cotton Blankets like This

400 Cotton Blankets like This

400 Cotton Blankets like This

= 400

= Bundle of Feathers

= 800 Bundles of Feathers

= 20

Bag of Dye Made = from the Cochineal Insect

= 40 Bags of Cochineal Dye

Another Kind of Warrior's Outfit (Headdress, Cotton armor, and shield)

This is part of a page from a record book kept by an Aztec tax collector. It shows how the Aztecs wrote with pictures and how they indicated numbers.

Aztec girls were trained to be quiet and shy. They never looked up if a man was near.

lake shore to the island of Mexico City. They constructed long aqueducts that brought in fresh drinking water. They raised flowers and used them by the thousands in ceremonies. Dignified officials carried bouquets as they went about their business. Aztecs were a people full of surprises. They were fearless warriors, and they practiced human sacrifice; but they loved beauty and were honest in their dealings with each other.

Unluckily for them, the Aztecs also liked trinkets made of gold. They collected great quantities of beads, necklaces, bells, plates, earplugs — whole treasure rooms full. When the Spaniards discovered this, they demanded and got an enormous amount of the treasure. The Aztecs gave it up peacefully because they felt superstitious awe of these strangers who seemed to be gods. But when Spanish soldiers attacked and killed every one of six hundred important Aztecs who had met for a religious ceremony, the warriors of Mexico City took up arms. A terrible war followed, and it did not end until the Spaniards had torn down nearly every building in the city, stone by stone.

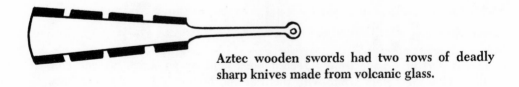

Aztec wooden swords had two rows of deadly sharp knives made from volcanic glass.

78

Aztec boys were trained to be soldiers. What looks like long winter underwear is really armor made of thick quilted cotton. Sometimes the armor had an extra coat of feathers sewed onto it.

Suppose It Had Been Different

Mexico City was powerful when the Spaniards destroyed it, but it was not very old. The Aztecs had grown rapidly on their well-protected island. They began there as a small, weak tribe. They ended up as rulers over nearly four hundred other cities and towns. What would have happened if the Spaniards had not come and conquered these conquerors? Would the Aztecs have kept their power? Would they have grown more and more civilized? Or would some of their victims have rebelled and become leaders in making new inventions and discoveries?

Of course, no one can be certain what would have happened. But, we do know that before Spanish times, Indians in Central America had made great progress. Surely, they could have gone right on to achieve much more, if invaders had not interrupted them.

Llamas

5

Adventure in the Andes

"I think I know where to find hidden gold that once belonged to an ancient Indian king." This is what an important man in Peru said one day to a young American named Hiram Bingham. Then he added, "Would you like to look for it?"

Bingham accepted the challenge. He loved adventure, and besides, he had studied history. He knew that the Inca Indians of Peru at one time really did have great treasures of gold. The Spaniards had seized much of this gold when they conquered Peru more than four hundred years ago, but they might have missed some of it. Maybe the Incas buried a hoard of their treasure in a secret place which the Spaniards never located.

The place that Bingham's Peruvian friend described certainly sounded promising. It was a ruined city named Cradle of Gold, high in the Andes Mountains and so hard to reach that only a dozen people had been there in the last hundred years.

Riding a mule, Bingham with his guides set out over a slippery mountain trail. Time and again, he looked helplessly down for thousands of feet as his mule teetered on the brink of a cliff. Once, high above a canyon bottom, an enormous bird called a condor attacked

Prehistoric Elephant Hunt

An Inca Ruler

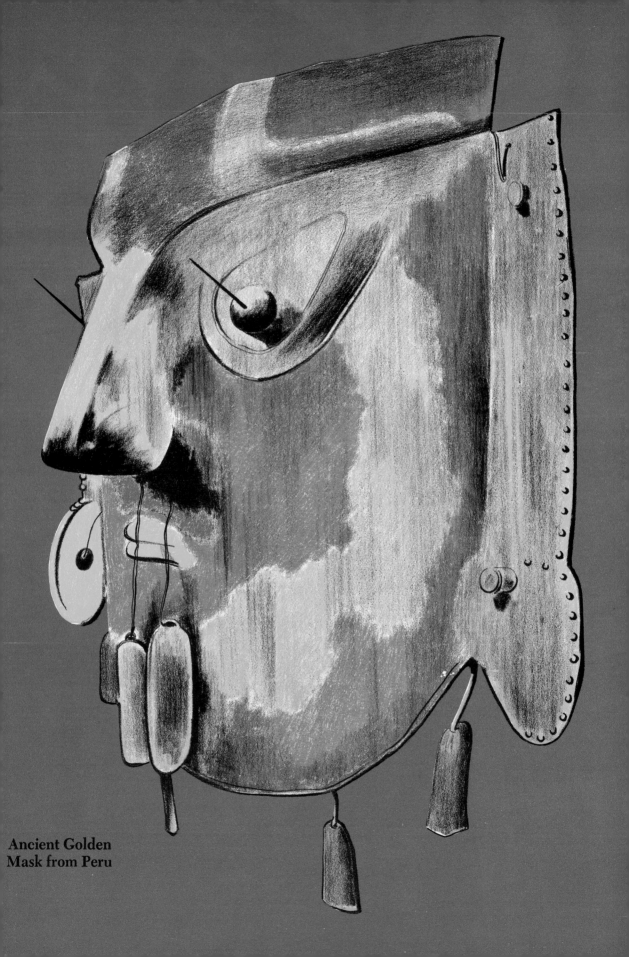

**Ancient Golden
Mask from Peru**

Painting in a
Mayan Temple
at
Bonampak, Mexico

Section from a Quipu

Incas had no written language. They remembered figures and facts with the help of knots in bundles of colored string. Such a bundle is called a quipu (KEY-poo). The type of knot reminded a quipu reader of one thing; the position of the knots reminded him of another; the color or length of a string made him remember still other things.

him and almost knocked him off into space. At last his guides led him into Cradle of Gold, and the hunt began.

It was a useless search. If treasure had ever been hidden here, someone else had found it.

The Peruvian was very disappointed, but not Bingham. He had found something more exciting to him than gold. He had discovered the fascination of looking for *anything* left by the ancient Incas. He had seen for himself that Peru was a large country with a great number of ruins waiting to be studied. There were mysteries to solve here, even a lost city to be traced.

After he went home to the United States, thoughts of this lost city filled Hiram Bingham's mind. He simply had to return to Peru and find it.

A Secret Hideaway

What was this city? How and why did it get "lost"?

To answer these questions we have to go back to the time when the Inca Indians ruled over their great empire in Peru. The Spaniards conquered most of this empire, but one Inca leader refused to give up. He moved into a secret city. Inca priests went with him to escape the Spaniards who were trying to stamp out the Indian religion. The Incas had an important temple in the secret city, and there they could perform their ceremonies in peace.

Of course, the Spaniards sent out spies and troops to look for the Inca hideaway, but they were always turned back before they actually reached it. Then the rebel leader died, and another took his place. At last the Spaniards were able to trick this new leader into leaving his capital, and they murdered him before he could return. But they still did not manage to find his headquarters.

With their leader gone, the Indians drifted away from the secret capital. In time they forgot about the place. As a matter of fact, the Incas forgot a great many things when they had to work as slaves for the Spaniards and could no longer work for themselves. After a while, no one repaired the wonderful Inca roads that ran for thousands of miles, linking all parts of the empire. Farmers stopped bringing food to the warehouses, which in the old days always held enough for everybody to eat. Now the craftsmen in the cities could not get food from the warehouses. With nothing to eat they had to stop working at their trades. Their skills died out. So did the knowledge of men called "rememberers" who kept track of all the crops, all the herds of llamas, all the cloaks, pots, sandals, and other useful products of the workshops in even the smallest town.

Inca civilization became as lost as the secret city that Hiram Bingham decided to look for.

Three Clues

Naturally, Bingham had clues which he thought would help him in his search. Some clues came from books written by the Spanish

82

The Incas built great swinging bridges across canyons. People paid a toll, not with money but with leaves of the century plant. The fibers from these leaves, twisted together, made ropes and cables for the bridges. The main cables were as thick as a man's body. For safety the caretaker replaced them every year.

invaders themselves. Others came from letters and papers that had belonged to their descendants. Still others came from books of history and legend written by men who were half Spanish and half Inca. Here are three of the many clues that seemed useful:

1. The lost city was in a place that Inca soldiers could easily defend. Which part of Peru seemed most likely? The waterless desert? The thick jungle? The mountains, almost unbelievably steep and hard to climb, with peaks that defenders could use as lookout points? Clearly *the lost city must be in the mountains.*

2. Spanish records said that, at one time, peanuts and parrot feathers had come from the lost city. Now it happens that peanuts and

parrots grow only in jungle country *east* of the mountains. Therefore, *the lost city must be in the eastern part of the mountains,* not too far from a supply of peanuts and parrots.

3. Old records mentioned windows in the lost city. This was intriguing. Inca buildings high in the mountains usually had few windows, or none at all, because it got very cold at night. Perhaps the buildings in the lost city had an unusual number of windows. Or perhaps the windows were unusual in size, or strange or interesting in shape. Bingham could not be exactly sure, but he hoped that this clue would help him recognize the lost city if he saw it.

The search started, and along the way more clues turned up. Bingham talked to people who lived on the eastern side of the mountains. Sometimes they guided him to ancient ruins, even to ruins that no archeologist knew about. But the particular lost city he sought still eluded him.

Then one day he went out with an Indian guide who said he knew the location of an ancient ruin. The river valley that they followed looked completely uninhabited. As they scrambled up a steep rocky hillside covered with a thick jungly growth, Bingham wondered if anyone had *ever* lived here. But he did not wonder long. He suddenly realized that the stones under the lush vegetation had been carefully shaped by man. Indeed, the stones formed walls for terraces on the mountainside. The terraces went up and up and up. This had been a huge garden of the kind that Incas often made on steep slopes. The people who tended it must have lived close by.

Bingham hurried from one terrace to the next. He climbed and climbed, until trees in the canyon bottom looked no bigger than blades of grass. And then, along a high ridge, he came upon a city, complete except that the stone buildings no longer had the grass roofs which once covered them. On two sides, mountain peaks guarded the city, and, on the other two sides, it was protected by steep canyon walls.

Here was a fortress that could be easily defended. It lay on the eastern side of the mountains, above the jungle areas where parrots and peanuts grew. Could this be the lost city he was looking for?

Bingham's excitement rose when he discovered a large stone sundial in perfect condition. This meant that the Spaniards had never been here. They always wrecked the sundials, which were a part of Inca religion. Bingham checked clue after clue. Everything seemed to fit. There were windows of a most unusual kind in the ancient temple. He was confident that he had located the lost city he had set out to find.

Other archeologists are not so sure. But they all agree about one thing: Hiram Bingham's search led him to a very important discovery. Never before had scientists been able to see an Inca city almost the way it was when the Indians lived in it long ago. The city is now called Machu Picchu (MAH-choo PEEK-choo), and the picture shows what it looks like.

Machu Picchu, the Lost City

Lost Highways

What would an explorer find if he followed the old Inca roads?

It took Victor von Hagen two exciting years to answer that question. No maps showed where the Incas had built their vast highway system. Von Hagen and his wife, Silvia, and other members of his expedition had to hunt for the roads. They used all the clues that could be found in the writings of the early Spaniards. They talked to descendants of the Incas who still live in the high mountains and the low valleys. They studied the landscape.

When a modern road followed the ancient one, the explorers travelled in a jeep and a truck, which also carried their supplies. Among the high peaks, they often had to leave these behind and ride horseback. Parts of the road consisted only of steps cut from solid rock. Here they had to go on foot. More than once they had to give up walking and take to a plane in order to catch a glimpse of the highway.

At times they camped in places higher than the highest peak in the Rocky Mountains. The air was so thin that they gasped for breath even when they were not moving, and they shivered for days at a time, although they were near the Equator. A few days later, they were sweltering in desert heat as they followed the road near the ocean.

In two years, Von Hagen and his companions explored much but not all of the highway system, which had a total length of more than 10,000 miles. One section of it ran for 3250 miles through the moun-

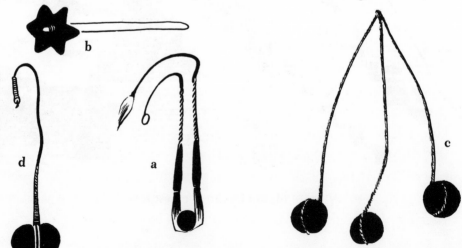

Inca soldiers used (a) slings, (b) war clubs, (c) bolas, and (d) big stone hammers with flexible handles.

Ancient Peruvians tied bundles of reeds together to make boats called balsas. Many balsas, lashed together side by side and covered with a thick mat of grass, formed a bridge.

tains from Quito (KEE-toe), Ecuador, to Talca (TAHL-kah) in Chile. That is longer than the distance from New York to San Francisco. At the time of the Incas, it crossed more difficult country than any other road in the world. It was one of the most amazing achievements of man.

Why did the Incas need this highway? In the beginning, it was a military road for huge armies that went out to conquer tribes not yet in the Empire. Later it was even more important. Taxes, food, work- men, messages — all sped along the roads toward the capital city of Cuzco (KOOS-koh). Officials, plans, orders — all sped out from the capital to the most distant villages.

The Incas were great organizers and great engineers. They built stone-walled terraces on countless, steep mountainsides to create farm- land where none had exisited before. The huge stones in the walls of their forts and temples fitted together perfectly, without any cracks or crevices between. Because of this absolutely tight fit, the builders did not have to use cement, and many walls are still standing after more than five hundred years. Even earthquakes have not loosened them.

One night, explorer Victor von Hagen and his wife took shelter in a cave. There they found company—the mummies of men who may have been Inca gold miners.

How were the Incas able to accomplish all this? For one thing, they inherited a great deal of knowledge from earlier people. These Old Ones of Peru left ruins and cemeteries in almost unbelievable numbers. Some archeologists find these earlier people even more interesting than the Incas.

Before the Incas Ruled

Archeologists used to work almost alone, except for a crew of unskilled helpers. If an explorer had a very lucky season he might make a sensational find, as Hiram Bingham did at Machu Picchu. But on a big project he usually had to work patiently year after year, slowly accumulating information. Other people had to wait a long time to get the benefit of any new facts he uncovered.

Nowadays, when there is money enough, archeologists work in teams. Where one man used to spend ten years digging, ten men spend one year. The team includes several different kinds of expert detectives, and they all get together to solve problems. Immediately, other people begin to share the benefit of what they find.

Not long ago, one of these streamlined, modern teams spent four months studying what had gone on in Peru *before* the days of the well-known Incas. The spot they chose was Viru Valley, one of many small valleys along the Pacific coast. The ten members of the team wasted no time tramping around looking for likely places to dig.

88

Instead, they studied big prints of photographs taken from an airplane. The photos showed ancient walls, mounds, canals — over a thousand places worth investigating. Archeologists dug into three hundred of these places. What they found, in addition to what they already knew, made a continuous story of Indian life in that one spot for an amazingly long time.

People of the Valley

The story begins 4500 years ago when a little band of hungry people wandered into Viru Valley and settled there. The river that ran down from the mountains gave them fresh water. In this part of Peru, it almost never rains and everything is desert except the river banks. The ocean provided fish and shellfish to eat, and the settlers raised gourds, squash, and peppers in the earth near the river. They did not know how to make clay pottery, but they used gourds for water bottles and even for cooking pots. To make water boil in a gourd, they dropped hot rocks into it. By doing this over and over, they could keep food stewing till it was cooked.

These first Viru Valley people also knew how to grow cotton, and they spun it into thread to make fish nets. Their only tools were stone axes and knives without handles. They had never heard of bows and arrows, and had very little need even for their spears. There were no big animals to hunt; no enemies disturbed them. Their houses were simply pits dug in the earth.

What did these shells reveal to scientists who found them buried in a garbage heap 4,000 years old? Turn the page and you will see.

One way and another, these early people got along. But life was hard. Every few years the ocean water suddenly warmed up. The fish that needed cool water died, and the people went hungry. There was no way of knowing why this or anything else happened. It just seemed that spirits made things behave in strange ways.

A small group of families stayed on and on in Viru Valley. All of them kept throwing away shells and fish bones and other refuse, and the pile grew higher and higher — a wonderful hoard of treasure waiting for future archeologists. Then, after thirteen hundred years of throwing away the same kind of trash, people began to toss out very different things — broken dishes.

At last someone, probably from the north, arrived in Viru Valley with corn and the knowledge of how to grow it. At the same time, the secret of making good clay cooking pots reached the valley. The strangers who taught the mysteries of corn and pottery also told about a mysterious kind of cat that had great power. If people pleased this cat-god, their lives would be easier.

The shells (on page 89) tell archeologists that some very good swimmers lived in Viru Valley. The shells come from a certain kind of mussel which grows only under water that is at least 15 feet deep.

A Vase in the Form of the Cat-god

This Viru Valley pot shows a soldier with shield and war club—or perhaps we should call him a sailor—sitting in a balsa boat. Boats just like it are still used in Peru.

It was obvious that corn farmers who believed in the cat-god did have better lives than the people who had no corn and little religion. Before long, the god's ugly face with huge terrible teeth appeared everywhere. People carved it in stone and modeled it in pots.

Life in Viru Valley became steadily better. More children grew up to raise families of their own. People built homes of mud bricks, and little clusters of houses grew into villages. Men cleared away thorn bush to make more fields. Now it was time to borrow another idea from nearby valleys: the farmers dug ditches and brought river water to their fields. Irrigation made their crops grow better than ever before.

By the year 1 A.D. Viru Valley had become important enough to attract enemies. The farmers took time to gather stones and pile them up into forts on hilltops. They also did what seemed necessary to get the protection of the cat-god. Inside the forts they piled sun-dried bricks into pyramids and built brick temples on top.

The next 500 years brought more and more changes. People now had a regular government. Impressive government buildings grew up around the cat-god's pyramids. In large brick apartment houses many families lived together, just as the Old Ones did in our own Southwest. The Viru Valley people entered their houses through the roofs, the way the Old Ones did.

But there were differences. In the Old Ones' homes the tiny rooms were all alike. In Viru Valley most of the rooms were small, but a few were large. Here some people had far more wealth than others. The poor did a great deal of work, building, building, building, and many skilled craftsmen made beautiful things to be buried with the rich when they died.

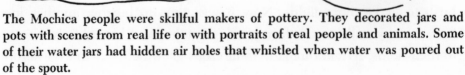

The Mochica people were skillful makers of pottery. They decorated jars and pots with scenes from real life or with portraits of real people and animals. Some of their water jars had hidden air holes that whistled when water was poured out of the spout.

92

Viru Valley people liked pots in the shape of animals.

Conquerors

All along the coast of Peru, rivers have cut many valleys. The people who lived in them traded, exchanged ideas, and fought each other. One day the Viru Valley walls were not strong enough to keep out a certain enemy — the warlike Mochica (moh-CHEE-kah) tribe from fifty miles to the north. The Mochicas ran Viru Valley in their own way for a long time.

Then, about the year 700 A.D., a different tribe came down from the mountains. These conquerors brought new ways of making pottery and new styles in home-building. They did not allow much to happen by chance. Instead, they planned and built better irrigation canals, bigger towns with streets arranged in careful order. Many families now had several rooms instead of just one.

These methodical warrior-builders captured other places along the seacoast, and they connected them all with a smooth, wide road. Then their rule, too, ended. Conquering armies came from the Kingdom of Chimu (chee-MOO) in the next valley.

The capital of Chimu was a fabulous city, called Chan-Chan, where a quarter of a million people lived. Many of them worked in factories and turned out great quantities of pottery jars, gold and silver

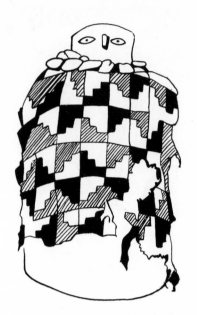

There is a human mummy inside this bundle which has a false head sewed on top. Ancient Peruvians often wrapped mummies in layers and layers of very fine, beautifully colored cloth. Between the layers they put things they thought would be useful in a future life—mantles and turbans, skirts and ponchos, feather fans, gold ornaments, water bottles, slingshots, and veils of delicate gauze.

vessels. Others made cloth, the best ever woven anywhere in the world until machinery was invented. Others worked with gadgets something like cookie cutters, stamping lavish decorations in wet mud on the city walls which were forty feet high.

The orderly life of the factory city did not spill over into conquered Viru Valley. Irrigation canals were neglected, and farmers moved away. At the same time, some people did learn how to do wonderful metal working, wood carving, and weaving for their rulers.

Then, about the year 1470, Inca armies conquered Chimu and overwhelmed Viru Valley. Close to the spot where naked Indians had once made their homes in pits, Incas built a palace with many rooms, a courtyard, and a lovely pool. Finally it, too, fell into decay after the Spaniards came, making the last addition to the ruins that archeologists have found so rich in information about Indian life.

The team of scientists who investigated Viru Valley had time to dig into only one promising spot out of every three on their map of the valley. Hundreds and hundreds of other fascinating places in Peru have not even been mapped yet. There is work here for whole generations of scientist-detectives still to do.

6

Ancient Engineers

How in the world did they do it?

How did Indians, long ago, manage to accomplish some of the tremendous things they did? Archeologists are not always sure, but they have worked out some theories.

How did ancient builders cut and shape huge blocks of stone? An abandoned quarry in Maya country gives one answer. For some reason, men stopped work in this quarry and went away, leaving their stone chisels and hammers and an example of every stage in their work.

First the stonecutters chiseled into solid rock until they had almost a whole block of it cut out. Then they used big wooden crowbars to break the block loose.

Quarry workers in Peru left unfinished jobs that reveal another ancient engineering trick. First they drilled a row of holes in the rock. Next they pounded dry wooden wedges into the holes. Then they drenched the wedges with water. The wood absorbed water, swelled up, and cracked the stone block free.

How did they move a huge block for miles and miles?

Often they used logs as rollers. Men pushed and pulled, the logs turned, and the block would slide forward. In at least one place, the Mayas may have slid big rocks along a road that was greased with slippery fresh mud.

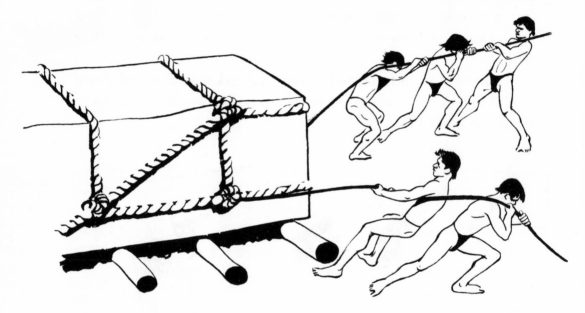

The Incas built tremendous stone walls without the help of any machinery. Archeologists figure that thirty thousand men must have labored for eighty years on the great fortress called Sacsahuaman (SAHK-sah-wah-MAHN) near Cuzco, the Inca capital. Many of the stones they used weighed twenty tons or more. The pictures show the way in which one expert thinks they may have moved some of the huge blocks:

(1) They set a post in the ground, then balanced a strong log on top of it so that the log could swing around without falling off. Next

they tied the big stone to one end of the log. On the other end of the log they tied bags. Into these they put stones that were small enough to be easily handled.

(2) The bags full of small stones at one end of the log finally balanced the big stone on the other end and lifted it off the ground — just the way several small girls on one end of a see-saw can lift up a large man on the other end.

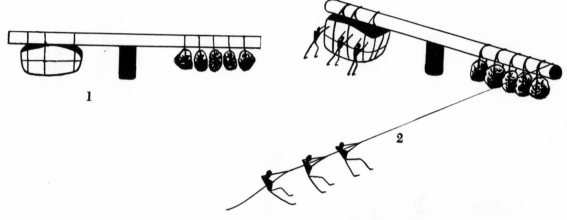

(3) When the big block was off the ground, men pulled on ropes and swung the log halfway around a circle. The big block had now changed places with the bags of little stones. The big block had been moved a whole log-length closer to the building site.

(4) Now the men untied the stones and let them rest on the ground. A new post was set up farther down the road. Again the men balanced the log on the post and repeated the whole process.

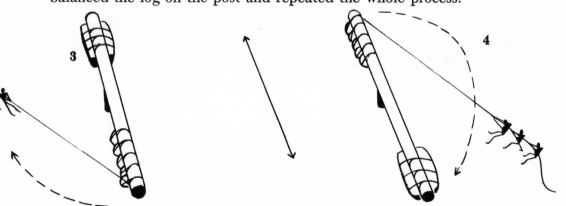

How did Indian builders manage to raise a big stone into position high above the ground?

They made a sloping roadway of earth up to the level where they wanted to put the stone. Then they hauled the stone up on rollers. When it was in position they removed the road! Archeologists know that this method was used in Peru because they found there an unfinished building with the sloping road still in position.

How did the Mayas set up a heavy stone column? Look at the pictures below.

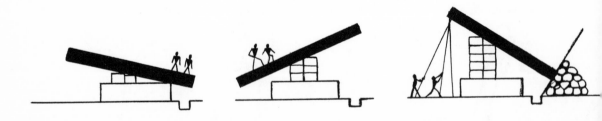

To make the column stand perfectly straight, they used a plumb bob, just as a modern builder does.

How did the Mayas build a roof over a room, using pieces of stone that were too small to reach from wall to wall?

On top of one wall they laid a row of stones which jutted out into the room. On top of the opposite wall they did the same thing. Then on these stones they kept laying row after row of stones which jutted out farther and farther until the front ends met over the center of the room.

A great deal of weight pressed down on the stones where they stuck out over empty space. To keep them from falling into the room, equal weight had to push down on the other ends of the stones. The builders piled up more masonry to do the balancing.

Engineers say a roof like this is built in the form of a *corbeled arch.* The Mayas also used this kind of arch in constructing stone bridges. So did the Incas.

The corbeled arch was a clever invention, but it had its disadvantages, too. A Mayan stone roof was tremendously heavy. In order to hold it up, the Mayas built thick walls. Thick walls meant small rooms. A Mayan temple, which was huge on the outside, had surprisingly little space inside. Nevertheless, simply by using small stones in a new way, people had learned how to do big things they could not do before.

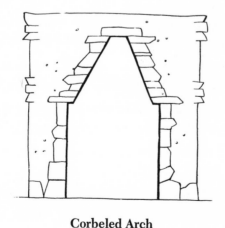

Corbeled Arch

7

Pyramids Close to Home

If you live in the eastern part of the United States, perhaps you have seen a certain kind of mound that hides a fascinating story. Some of these mounds are shaped like half an orange with the flat side down. Others are walls of earth in the shape of circles or squares. Still others will seem to have no special form of any kind — until you fly over them in an airplane. Then you may discover that they look like giant snakes or birds or bears. Whatever the shape, all these mounds were made long ago. Men and women and children carried endless basketfuls of earth until they had piled up the form they wanted. When baskets wore out, they were dropped on the heap, and the prints remained there for archeologists to discover hundreds of years later.

Many of the mounds are flat-topped pyramids. They resemble the temple pyramids of Mexico, except that they are not covered with hard plaster and rock, and they have no stone temples on top. Did North American Indians make temple pyramids *without temples?* No, the buildings have simply disappeared. But archeologists know what many of them looked like and can draw pictures of them. Some were circular. Some had square corners. The framework was made of wooden posts. For the walls, branches from trees or canes that grew in marshy places were woven in and out among the upright posts, then covered with mud. Bundles of grass covered the roofs.

Naturally, buildings like this did not last long. How then can an archeologist know about them? He finds their ghosts! He finds them hidden in the earth on top of the pyramids. With a shovel or trowel he shaves off one thin layer of earth at a time and watches for any change

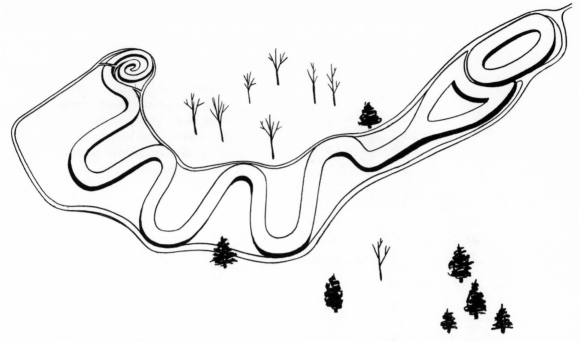

This is one of the mounds of earth that prehistoric Indians built in Ohio. It resembles a huge snake a quarter of a mile long. Before the builders started piling up the mounds, they outlined its shape with rows of stones. Snakes were sacred creatures in many parts of the Americas, and this Serpent Mound must have had a religious meaning.

in the color of the ground where he is working. A roundish, dark spot in lighter-colored clay tells him he is on the track of his ghost. Many dark spots in a circle, or a square, mean he has found it.

Each dark spot betrays the place where a post once stood. The temple's wooden framework has disappeared, but you can see the marks of post holes in the earth, *no matter how long ago they were made.*

Inside the phantom walls of a building, the archeologist uncovers the remains of an ancient fire pit. Open fires under grass roofs had just the result you would expect. They sometimes set buildings ablaze. Experts have been lucky enough to find places where the fire smoldered slowly, leaving charcoal instead of ashes. Now charcoal, unlike wood, never decays. This means that charred pieces of cane or bunches of grass will last for centuries, if they are protected so that water does not wash them away.

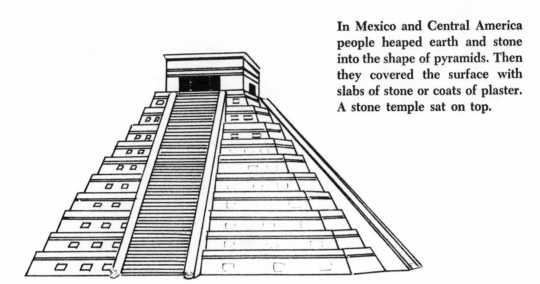

In Mexico and Central America people heaped earth and stone into the shape of pyramids. Then they covered the surface with slabs of stone or coats of plaster. A stone temple sat on top.

In North America, along some of the great rivers, people followed the same custom, but they did not build with stone. This pyramid was plastered with mud and had steps made of logs. The temple was built of poles and woven reed mats.

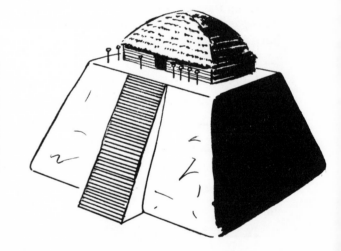

How does a bunch of charred grass prove that a temple had a grass-covered roof? All by itself, of course, it does not prove any such thing. But think about the discovery that archeologist Glenn A. Black made at the large Angel Mound on the bank of the Ohio River in Indiana. He was examining the remains of burned buildings when he noticed some ancient nests of the mud dauber wasp. These nests were made of clay. Strangely, they had not dissolved on the wet ground where they had been lying for centuries. Instead, their shapes were still perfect, and the reason for this was odd. The clay had been baked in fire — hardened like pottery.

Black knew that mud dauber wasps fasten their nests tightly under a sheltered place, such as the roof of a building. He looked carefully. Sure enough, marks in his baked, mud nests showed what they had been attached to: grass — grass roofs.

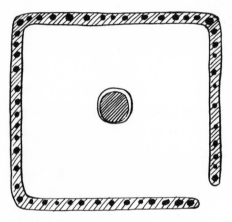

When archaelogists dig up a mound, they work so carefully that they can discover spots in the earth where wooden posts once stood. A map of the post holes reveals the shape of a building.

Putting together the post hole map and many other clues, an archeologist can tell what the ancient building looked like.

The Mayas Again

Who built these grass-roofed temples on top of pyramids? The Mayas? They could have paddled in canoes all the way along the coast of the Gulf of Mexico, then up North American rivers. Or did some other Indians from Mexico come northward on foot, and continue their temple building in the fertile lands that they found?

In many places Indians used mounds as cemeteries. These drawings show how a group of people in Illinois were buried in a small stone room which was then roofed with logs and covered with a big mound of earth.

Nobody knows yet whether Mayas or other Mexican Indians actually moved into southeastern United States. But their temple-building *idea* certainly did spread. Perhaps traders brought it. Perhaps warriors or prisoners of war carried the idea northward gradually from one tribe to another. At any rate, it did reach a long way up the great rivers into the very heart of North America. In dozens of villages, Indians heaped up pyramids of earth to lift their places of worship toward the sky.

Temple pyramids are not the only evidence of a link with Mexico. Other clues have appeared, too. Can you see any clues in the two sets of pictures on this page and the next? Aztecs in Mexico made one set. North American Indians made the others. The North American decorations were carved on shell and buried in an important person's grave at a place called Spiro in eastern Oklahoma.

Eagle Dancer Drawn by a Mound Builder

Eagle Dancer Drawn by an Aztec

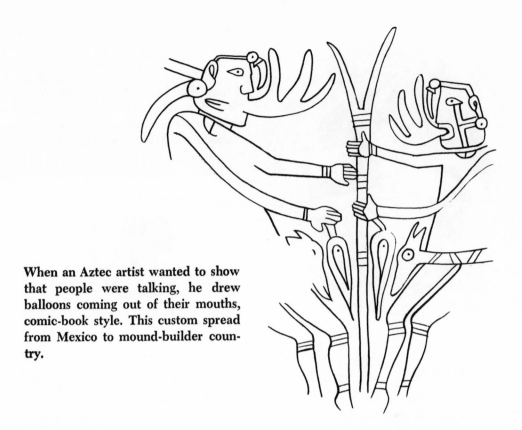

When an Aztec artist wanted to show that people were talking, he drew balloons coming out of their mouths, comic-book style. This custom spread from Mexico to mound-builder country.

The drawing on the left was made by an Aztec. The one above was made by a mound builder.

It certainly looks as if the Spiro artists borrowed from Mexico. But at the same time, they were doing things in their own way. The two men in the large picture are choosing up sides for a special ball game which Indians in the United States invented. The game was played by huge teams — fifty or more on a side. A player used two racquets that looked like long-handled kitchen strainers. With them he tried to scoop up a small, leather ball and make a goal with it.

105

A mound-builder artist drew this picture of a man playing a game of chunkey with a stone that has been rounded and polished so that it would run smoothly over the ground.

Chunkey Stone

What happened to the ball-playing builders of temple mounds? A good clue comes from the game, itself, and also from another game called chunkey. (You can see a chunkey stone in the hand of the man in the circular picture.) Although the grass-roofed temples disappeared, these sports lived on. Creek Indians were still playing them when European settlers first moved westward across this country.

Another clue comes from an old book written by an early Spanish explorer. He actually saw Creeks and other Indians holding ceremonies in temples on the tops of pyramids. The ceremonies died out; the temples vanished; but the people remained. They were the ancestors of Indians still living today.

In Mexico and Central America people used three-legged pots. The fashion spread to North America. The pot on the left came from a mound in Illinois.

Mounds Full of Bones

The first real efforts to learn the secrets of an Indian mound were made by Thomas Jefferson, a man who had enormous curiosity — a true scientist. The mound he investigated, near his home in Virginia, was rounded and not as big as most temple pyramids. Jefferson dug carefully all the way to the center of it, making detailed notes of everything he found. What he unearthed was a cemetery filled with the bones of a thousand people.

Later, archeologists investigated many other burial mounds all over the East. On a farm called Hopewell near Chillicothe, Ohio, they found one that contained very beautiful objects. These were different from anything the temple mound builders made, and the mound, itself, turned out to be much older. Now whenever a mound resembles the one near Chillicothe, it is called a Hopewell, and there are many of them. From Hopewell graves come fine pottery, ornaments hammered out of copper, tobacco pipes carved from stone, often in the

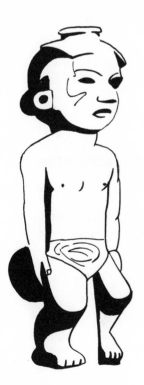

The Hopewell people had neighbors who are known as Adena people. Here are three things that Adenas made: a pipe carved in the shape of a man, a point for a weapon, and a decoration in the shape of a bird.

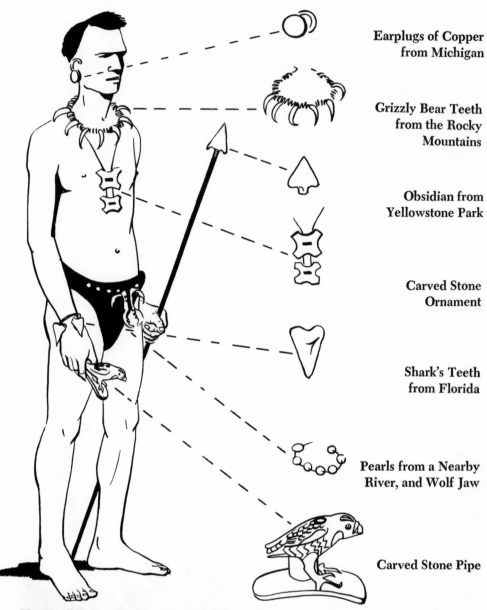

Earplugs of Copper from Michigan

Grizzly Bear Teeth from the Rocky Mountains

Obsidian from Yellowstone Park

Carved Stone Ornament

Shark's Teeth from Florida

Pearls from a Nearby River, and Wolf Jaw

Carved Stone Pipe

Hopewell men, who lived in the valley of the Ohio River, were fine craftsmen. They made ornaments and weapons and tools from materials that came from many distant places.

shapes of animals. A grave in one mound was blanketed with large pearls — 60,000 of them. Another held more than a hundred pipes. Another contained little statuettes showing how the Hopewells actually looked.

108

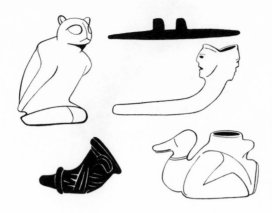

In many Indian tribes, men smoked pipes during their ceremonies. The pipes were made of stone, bone, or clay.

Often, a man was buried wearing a necklace of grizzly bear teeth. How did these teeth get to Ohio? Grizzlies lived in the Rockies, not the Midwest. There were obsidian spear points, too, although the nearest obsidian mines were in Yellowstone Park. Sea shells from Florida and Alabama also turned up, and copper from Michigan and mica from the mountains to the east. Some experts think the Hopewells were great traders. Others think that perhaps they sent out special expeditions for things they wanted.

In one way or another, Hopewell artists got great quantities of material that they turned into beautiful decorations. They hammered copper nuggets into thin sheets, which they cut and shaped to make helmets, earplugs, ornamental buttons. Mica was something that they made into lovely objects found nowhere else. From large perfect sheets of it they cut silhouettes of hands, heads, eagle claws. These, along with all the other ornaments a person collected in his lifetime, were for use on the journey he expected to take after he died.

At Poverty Point, in lower Mississippi, archeologists found countless blobs of pottery like these. Turn the page to find out what they were.

In ancient times Indian women often cooked food by dropping hot stones into vessels made of wood or bark or skin, which could not be put directly onto the fire. At Poverty Point there were no stones. That is why the women made artificial cooking stones from clay, which hardened when baked in the fire.

The Hopewells seemed to spend their whole, colorful lives getting ready to die. Why was this?

Nobody really knows. Nobody knows very much yet about some other things. For instance, archeologists have found signs of a people, very different from the Hopewells, who lived at the same time and throughout the same area. Who were they? We do not have the final answer by any means. But we do know that a great number of fascinating things went on in the distant past among the Indians of America's woodlands — far more things than anyone used to dream of.

Why did many of the activities of Hopewell times come to an end? Why did the great skills of the Hopewells disappear? What happened to these fine carvers in stone and workers in copper? Who were the Hopewells anyway and where did they come from?

Archeologists are busy looking in the earth for clues that will lead them to the answers.

8

Looking for the First Indian

After the cowboy Richard Wetherill discovered Cliff Palace, he spent the rest of his life trying to track down the Old Ones. Who were they? Where did they come from? Before the Old Ones, there were Older Ones who were fine basket makers. Wetherill found out that much, but the discovery only led to more questions. Where did the Older Ones come from — and when?

This is the way with discoveries. Each time a question is answered, a new one pops up. Archeologists who are looking for the whole story of human life in the Americas keep going further and further back into the past.

Where did any Indians anywhere, anytime, come from? *How long ago?*

Scientists know that the ancestors of all people were some kind of apelike creature. We know that people have been on this earth for hundreds of thousands of years, but nobody has found a single sign that apelike creatures ever lived in the Americas. That leaves the Indians without any ancestors — unless they came from Europe or Africa or Asia. We had better rule out Europe and Africa, scientists decided. It was too hard for ancient man to reach America from either of these two continents.

That left Asia as the earlier home of the Indians.

How long had Indians been in America? The question had no sure answer. But in 1926 a Negro cowboy named George McJunkin found something that gave an important clue.

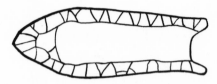

(2) A Folsom Point Actual Size

(1) **Prehistoric Bison Ribs with a Spear Point Stuck Between Them, Found near Folsom, New Mexico**

(3) **How the Point Was Attached to the Shaft of a Spear**

McJunkin was following a trail left by a stray steer a few miles from the little cow town of Folsom, New Mexico. At one point, he noticed something unusual in the steep side of an arroyo. Very large bones were sticking out, and they looked as if they had been buried underneath about twelve feet of earth. The cowboy swung out of the saddle and picked up two things that resembled arrowheads lying among the bones. These were not like any arrowheads he had ever come across before. They had long hollow grooves in each side.

Sometime later, in the town of Raton, McJunkin told two ranchers about the big bones and the strange arrowheads. The ranchers took a look for themselves, then wrote to J. D. Figgins, a museum man who was interested in old bones. Figgins got really excited. These bones came from a huge kind of straight-horned bison that died out thousands of years ago. Was it possible that the strange, grooved arrowheads had actually been shot into this extinct beast? If so, the cowboy's discovery would be of tremendous importance. It would *prove* that men had been in America a very long time indeed.

Figgins lost no time in arranging to have more bones dug out. The digging had to continue, off and on, for two years before he found

112

just what he needed — a flint point and bison bones, right next to each other in the earth.

Now Figgins stopped work and sent telegrams to important museums. As fast as trains could bring them, three experts came from the East. They saw the flint point lying between two rib bones and were convinced. Someone had, indeed, poked a spear into one of the extinct bison a very long time ago. Because the first signs of this ancient hunter were found near the little town of Folsom, he was called Folsom Man, and the sharp-edged flint tips he made for his spears were named Folsom points.

How old was Folsom Man? Some said only 3,500 years. Others thought he was much older. Nobody really knew. But surely if men hunted and killed animals, now extinct, at one place in those far-off days, they must have done so at other places. Archeologists began an eager search.

No archeologist has yet found the skeleton of any hunter who made Folsom points. But scientists have found the remains of ancient bison and can tell us what the great animals looked like.

More Evidence

In 1930, M. R. Harrington found some promising clues in Gypsum Cave near Las Vegas, Nevada. On the cave's dry floor lay animal droppings that were very big and not like those of any creature living today. *Underneath* the droppings were spear points and well-preserved, wooden spear shafts. This meant that some animal had stayed in the cave *after* men lived there. But what big animal was built so that it could crawl through the small openings between one part of the cave and another? Only one that Harrington could think of — the giant ground sloth which had been extinct for a very long time.

Harrington mailed packages of the ancient droppings to experts in various museums and asked for identification. Presently word came back. The animal was certainly a giant ground sloth!

Here was evidence that human beings had been in America a good long time, and the cave had still more evidence to offer. Man-made objects and bones from extinct American camels were found together, *under* the remains of the giant ground sloth.

Two years later an archeologist was working near Dent, Colorado. There he found spear points mixed in among the bones of still another

This spear point found in Gypsum Cave was used as a weapon against the giant ground sloth.

114

This is called a Clovis point. It was often used to kill huge elephants called mammoths.

animal that had disappeared long ago — the huge kind of prehistoric elephant called the mammoth. These spear points had their own very definite shape.

In the next few years, more points of the same kind were found in a gravel pit near Clovis, New Mexico, and they came to be known as Clovis points. Here they were sometimes mixed with the bones of extinct bison, but they were also found near mammoth bones.

Many of these Clovis points had grooves down the middle. (Archeologists say they were "fluted.") The flutes resembled the flutes in Folsom points, but were shorter. You can easily tell the difference.

There was another difference. Folsom Man, it seemed, did not hunt mammoths. At least, none of his delicately shaped bits of flint had ever been found with mammoth bones. What did this mean?

Archeologists began to suspect that Clovis points were older than Folsom points. They hoped to find something in the Clovis gravel pit that would tell them whether this hunch was right. Then came the villain. A souvenir hunter spied a small Folsom point in one of the upper levels of the gravel pit. The point was stuck in a piece of bone. He dug it out, tossed the bone aside, and went away with a new point for his collection.

When archeologists heard the story, it was too late to do anything but groan. A thoughtless collector had spoiled important evidence. Scientists would just have to keep on hoping for another chance to check their theory that Clovis points were older than Folsom points.

Camels in Nevada

In the meantime, another scientist made a find at Tule Springs, forty miles from Gypsum Cave in Nevada. Here was charcoal buried way down deep, along with bones of animals, including a large kind of camel, called Camelops, which used to roam over much of this country. The bones had been cooked and split open for the marrow they contained. Surely, this was a very early campsite of very early man. The best evidence of all was a flake of obsidian that lay among the ashes. This flake bore certain tiny marks proving that men had chipped it from a bigger piece of stone purposely to use as a tool.

Now the scientist wanted experts to see his discovery. He dug out of the earth a solid block that held obsidian, charcoal, and bone and shipped it to the American Museum of Natural History in New York. Yes, the experts agreed, this was important evidence that men had been in America ages ago.

But *when* — in what century — did hunters in Nevada dine on Camelops? There were guesses, but they varied by thousands of years. No one really knew.

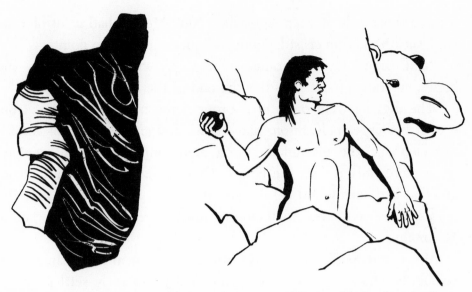

Most people would think that this was just an ordinary chunk of rock. But scientists who studied it found that it was shaped on purpose by a human being who used it as a tool. The tool was found along with charcoal from a campfire and the bones of a kind of camel that used to live in America.

Sandia Cave

One spring day in 1936, some Boy Scouts who were out hiking discovered a cave in the mountains east of Albuquerque, New Mexico. A rock slide at some time in the past had cut off any trail to the cave, but the boys found a way in. On the cave floor they saw bits of Indian pottery.

Before long, news of the discovery came to archeologist Frank Hibben. He climbed up for a look. Every step he took in the cave raised clouds of choking dust, but what he managed to see interested him a good deal.

Hibben dug in the cave during four summers. There he found Indian history arranged in the neat layers an archeologist always dreams of finding, but seldom does. In the top layer were potsherds and a few tools left by the Old Ones — the ancient Pueblo Indians.

Under the first layer, Hibben struck a thin crust of rock that had been made by water dripping from the cave roof. It must have been

117

formed thousands of years ago when New Mexico had a lot of rain. Underneath the thin crust lay animal bones and Folsom points.

Next came a layer of orange-colored clay with nothing in it — no bones, no Indian tools. Was this the end of the line?

The digging went on, and it brought rewards: more bones from extinct horses, camels, bison, mammoths, and another kind of American elephant, the mastodon. Much more important were nineteen spear points mixed with the bones. These points were different from any that had been found before, and the name, Sandia (san-DEE-ah) points, has been given to them because the cave is in the Sandia Mountains.

When did Sandia Man live? An astonishing answer came from geologists who studied the cave. Apparently this early settler was in New Mexico 15,000 or 20,000 years ago.

Prospecting for Bones

Archeologists often turned to geologists for help as they searched for ancient man in America. Near Mexico City, in 1947, Helmut de Terra put a new geological gadget to work prospecting for mammoth bones. He thought that if he found the bones, he might also find some evidence of men who hunted the huge creatures.

De Terra knew that the remains of eight mammoths had already been discovered by workers who were digging a ditch near the village of Tepexpan (TAY-paysh-PAHN). The spot where the bones lay deeply buried had once been the swampy shore of a lake. It was hard for De Terra to believe that so many mammoths had just wandered

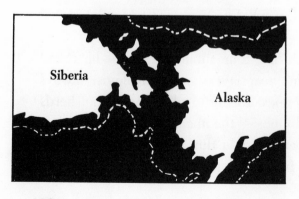

How did ancient man come to the Americas? Thousands of years ago Alaska and Siberia were joined together by land, and people wandered freely from Asia into North America.

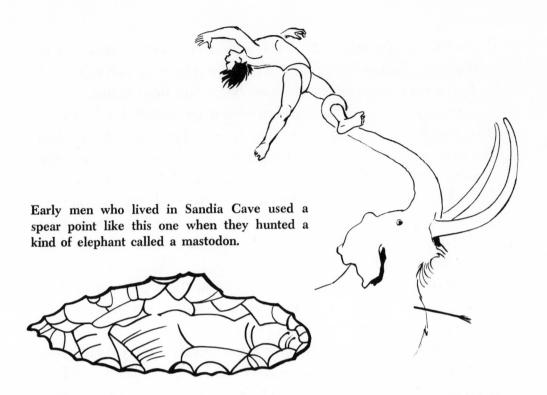

Early men who lived in Sandia Cave used a
spear point like this one when they hunted a
kind of elephant called a mastodon.

into the water and died by accident. More likely, men had stampeded
the heavy animals to this swampy place where they would bog down
and be easy to kill.

If that was what happened, there might be some more mammoth
skeletons along the ancient lake shore. And if there were more skeletons, there might be a spear point or knife near one of them.

All this was very "iffy." Besides, no trace of the bones could be
seen on the surface. But it was impossible to dig up the whole large
area. De Terra needed some way of looking down through several feet
of earth without moving it. He wanted X-ray eyes.

Science could not offer these, but geologists did have an invention
that would let him listen through rock. This gadget sent a current of
electricity into the earth, and at the same time it was connected to
earphones. A man wearing the earphones could tell by the sound
whether the current was traveling smoothly or meeting obstacles.

De Terra listened, hoping to hear obstacles—and hoping the obstacles would be elephant bones. He did hear bones. But to his delight,

and to the amazement of the whole world, the bones turned out to be those of a human being instead of an elephant! A man's skeleton lay in the same layer where elephant bones had been found.

Newspapers all over the world printed stories about this Tepexpan Man. People in Germany knew that he was between fifty-five and sixty-five years old, when he drowned in the same swamp where the mammoths had perished. People in London knew that a dentist, who X-rayed the old fellow's teeth, said he must have suffered a great deal from toothache. Everyone was interested in Tepexpan Man. He seemed much more real than Folsom Man or Sandia Man whose skeletons had not yet been found.

How long ago did Tepexpan Man live in the Valley of Mexico? Geologists gave as close an answer as they could. They said he lived *about* 11,000 years ago.

They had to say *about*. Nobody knew exactly. Nobody knew the *exact* age of any of the clues to ancient man. Then in the year 1950 a marvelous discovery was announced. Atomic scientists had invented a test for elephant tusks, or wood, or charcoal, or bones that would tell exactly how old they were, give or take a few years.

This test is very complicated—and very expensive. The equipment for making it looks like something from a science fiction story. But, if archeologists can get money to have the work done, they can now send a sample of plant or animal material to the atomic laboratory, and back will come a date.

Every single thing that was once alive has a built-in calendar, which the atomic scientist can read. Material that archeologists once threw away as useless suddenly became valuable. A chunk of charcoal now could be more precious than a magnificent tomb filled with gold.

This new way of telling age is called carbon dating or radiocarbon dating or simply C 14 dating. Now let us see if we can keep up with atomic detectives as they leap from one C 14 date to another, far into the distant past.

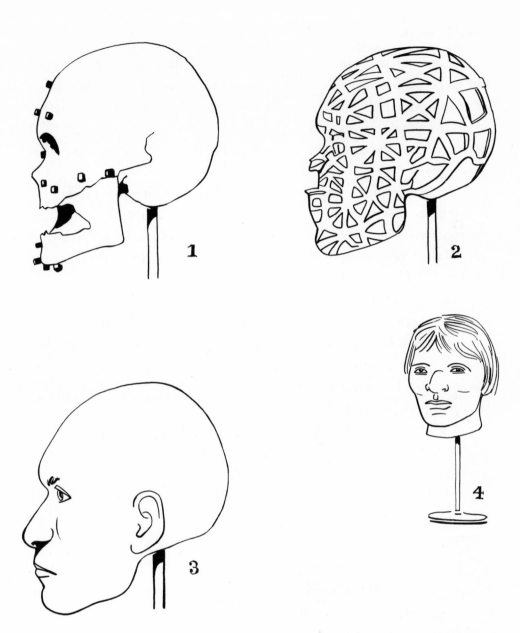

Some sculptors can make a recognizable portrait of you without ever seeing you or even your photograph. All they need is a lot of accurate measurements of your head. These same sculptors can measure ancient skulls and then model heads and faces that show what prehistoric people must have looked like. These drawings show (1) a model of Tepexpan man's skull, with knobs on which the sculptor will begin to build up the face; (2) partly built-up face; (3) side view without hair; (4) finished head.

Date Detection

A piece of shell from a Hopewell burial mound in Ohio turned out to be 2285 years old. Farther north, in Wisconsin, are the graves of people who, like the Hopewells, worked with copper. Carbon-dated wood from their graves tells us they lived 7150 years ago. Another C 14 date says that Indians were at the farthest tip of South America 8500 years ago.

Charcoal from southern Nebraska proves that men lived along the Republican River nearly 9,000 years ago. This charcoal came from the top layer of a refuse heap. How old is the bottom layer? We may never know, because nobody collected any material from it that could be dated. And now a dam has flooded the place.

You remember the cave in New Mexico where early people left a great number of sandals? It was not the only one of its kind. Fort Rock Cave in Oregon contained nearly a hundred sandals protected from decay by ash that sifted in after a volcano erupted. How old were the sandals? The atomic calendar in the sagebrush bark from which they were woven says 9050 years.

At Plainview, Texas, 9170 years ago, men killed a great many bison. About 200 years before that date, other bison hunters camped near the now Angostura Reservoir in South Dakota.

And what about Folsom Man, the bison hunter whose spear points sent archeologists on a great search for the earliest American? Carbon

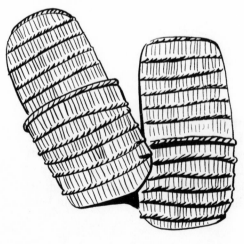

A carbon 14 dating machine, like the one shown on the next page, tells us that these sandals are about 9,000 years old.

122

14 tests of bones found with Folsom points set their age at 10,780 years.

While Folsom Men were killing the oversized bison that used to roam the Great Plains, other men were living quieter lives farther east. These people gathered seeds and roots, hunted deer, and took shelter under a ledge at Modoc, Illinois. How long ago? About 10,000 years.

At about this same time, hunters lived in Gypsum Cave in Nevada.

C 14 dates agree with the geologists about Tepexpan Man. He must have been hunting mammoths at least 11,000 years ago in Mexico. At several places in the United States, other men killed the big animals a thousand years before that.

From mammoths, the C 14 trail leads to the camels which men roasted at Tule Springs. Charcoal from their fire gave an astonishing date. It was *more than 23,800 years old.* We do not know how much more because the equipment that tested the charcoal did not work for dates that were any older.

Then scientists developed a more sensitive test, and they tried it on two sets of strange, charred bones. These bones came from Santa

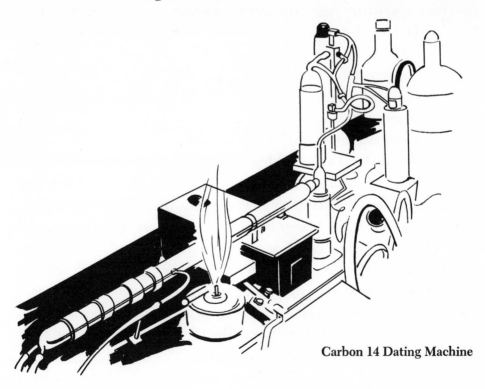

Carbon 14 Dating Machine

About 7,000 years ago people near the Great Lakes found big lumps of pure copper which they pounded into spear points like this. Copper chunks exist in very few places. That is why early men had to use stone spear points.

Rosa Island, a small bit of land that long ago got separated from California by a strip of ocean. Now a curious thing happened to the mammoths that lived on Santa Rosa. They changed and became a special dwarf breed. Men occasionally killed the creatures, and bones found at one of their campfires indicated that they feasted on dwarf mammoth steak 15,500 years ago. Hold your hat when you see the figure for the C 14 test on the other set of bones from a different Santa Rosa campfire. They were 27,150 years old at the very least!

Before anyone could get used to the idea that people have lived in America for so many years, the atomic scientists made more improvements in the tests. Into the dating machine went a bit of charred wood from a gravel bed at Lewisville, Texas. The wood came from a place where men camped, built a fire and, apparently, dropped one of their big spear tips—the kind called a Clovis point. But when the C 14 test date came from the laboratory, nobody could believe it. The wood from Lewisville was at least *37,000 years old.*

Archeologists tried again with a different piece of charcoal from a different fire pit in the same Lewisville gravel bed. The report was the same. Experts are still scratching their heads over this. They find it hard to believe that the Clovis point is 37,000 years old. That would make it the oldest chipped-stone spear point ever found anywhere in the world. Does this mean that men in America discovered how to make spear points before the art of chipping stone had developed anywhere else in the world? Or does it mean simply that somebody made a mistake about the spot where the Clovis point was found? Or was there a mistake in the dating test?

124

Someday experts may discover more facts about the age of Clovis points. Meanwhile, we know this much: human beings got off to a very slow start in their efforts to build a good life for themselves in America, or anywhere else, for that matter.

At first, very long periods of time went by between one invention and another. A man might think up a new tool, and then hundreds or thousands of years might pass before another man improved it. But people did make changes. They did create new tools to help them meet the new conditions they found in various places at different times. And the more they invented, the easier it was to invent still more.

For example, think of the C 14 dating method. Scientists invented a complicated, atomic dating machine, and almost overnight they found a way to improve it. Then, while this book was being written, inventors announced that they had several new and entirely different ways of finding out how old an object is.

But do not get the idea that just because we have more and more tests we will keep on finding older and older dates for man in America. We may never find *any* dates older than the ones we already have. The new tests should help us, though, to get dates that are *more accurate*. They will also make it possible to tell the age of a greater variety of things. And every new, exact date we get for anything in man's past will help us put together more of the story of man's long struggle to become master of the world he lives in.

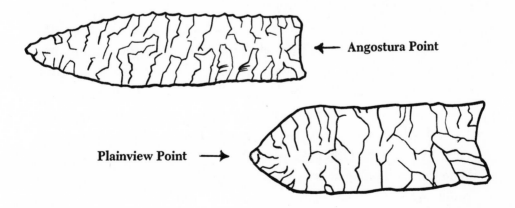

← Angostura Point

Plainview Point →

9

Mysteries Still To Be Solved

The first Americans were great inventors of gadgets. They had knife sharpeners, arrow straighteners, hole punchers, pot smoothers, hair tweezers, hundreds of little things that made work easier or weapons better or life more interesting. You can tell by looking at some of these gadgets just what they were used for. Others are real puzzlers. Many a mysterious object still has not been figured out.

What would you think if you discovered polished stone things like those at the top of the next page? They have turned up by the dozen in eastern United States. For a while everybody was satisfied to call them bannerstones, because they resembled the ornaments which people often put on the tops of poles that held banners or flags. Indian chiefs or priests were supposed to have carried the ornaments at ceremonies. But archeologist Arthur Parker had his doubts. He suspected that his ancestors, the Seneca Indians, had used the stones in a more practical way. Did a bannerstone on the end of a long wooden spear have the same effect as feathers on an arrow? Could it give the spear a longer, steadier flight? Parker experimented and found to his satisfaction that it did.

But evidence found in an ancient grave in Kentucky indicated a different use. There a bannerstone was attached to a spear thrower, which is sometimes called an atlatl.

Men who hunted with atlatls also made hundreds of beautiful little objects that looked like statues of birds. Some of the statues had popeyes, some did not. What were these birdstones for? One guess seemed as good as another: basket handles, canoe ornaments, headdress decorations, pipe holders, knife handles. Finally, a birdstone was discovered which convinced many people that it was a finger grip fastened to an atlatl. Other people still say they just do not know.

When an archeologist is not sure about an object he often calls it a "problematical." The pictures on page 130 show several small

126

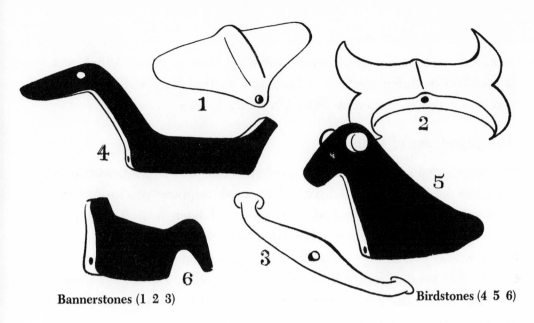

Bannerstones (1 2 3)   **Birdstones (4 5 6)**

problematicals. There are whopping big ones, too. In Costa Rica, for instance, archeologists have come upon great round stone balls lying about the jungle. Some of them are eight feet in diameter; hundreds of others vary in size down to a few inches. Who carved them so perfectly? Why?

Desert Geometry

Another giant puzzle was studied by Paul Kosok, when he flew in a plane over Nazca on the coast of Peru. Looking down, he saw what nobody on the ground would suspect. The desert resembled a page in some vast geometry book! There were straight lines, miles long, meeting at angles. Other lines seemed to make rectangles, triangles. Kosok wondered if ancient astronomers drew the figures, perhaps in order to help them tell the changes in the seasons. But why did they make the figures so vast when small ones would do as well? Some other marks in the sand were even more mysterious. They appeared to be huge drawings of animals. What artist made them? When? Why?

At Tres Cruces (TRAYSS KROO-sayss), another place on the coast of Chile, ancient artists scooped out trenches in a sandy hillside, making an enormous picture which could be seen from far off. Since rain almost never falls in that part of the world, the drawing has lasted for hundreds and hundreds of years. But what does it show? What was it for? Did boatmen use it as a landmark so that they would not get lost along the monotonous shore? Nobody knows.

The Importance of Holes

Suppose you dug into a very ancient house in the Southwest and found in the floor a pit filled with clean sand. Suppose you saw in the sand a few stones that looked as if they had been heated in a fire, although there was no charcoal or other sign of a fire inside the house. What would you think? Archeologists believe that some clever home builder got tired of living in a room full of smoke. He heated stones in a fire *outside* the house, then dropped them into the sand pit inside the house, and thus invented a radiator.

But the Old Ones in the Southwest also dug similar pits in kiva floors. These apparently were not radiators because kivas had special fire pits. Some of the problematical holes were covered with stone slabs. Were they used in ceremonies? How? Did dancers drum on the stone slabs with their feet?

At Machu Picchu, Hiram Bingham found curious round holes bored into a stone wall. The openings widened to form small chambers about the right size for a snake to curl up in. The Incas sometimes carved snakes into the stone over doorways. Did they also think it was good luck to offer the creatures a home in the wall?

Why? Why? Why?

Another custom at Machu Picchu seems puzzling. For the most part this was a very tidy city, but at one spot near the sun temple the Incas left a huge pile of potsherds. Did they break dishes there on purpose? In Central America, archeologists have found carvings, statues of gods, even whole buildings that were deliberately smashed. Why? Far away in northeastern United States, people smoked stone pipes carved in the shapes of animals. Archeologists have noticed that they almost never find a whole owl-shaped pipe. For some strange reason, these birds' heads were carved and then cut off.

128

The meaning of this giant design on a mountainside on the coast of South America is an unsolved mystery.

Were all three of these customs part of people's religious beliefs? Why?

When Earl Morris and his wife Ann were digging in an ancient cliff dwelling, they discovered a puzzle that no one has been able to solve: a grave that contained two human forearms and hands, no other part of a body. Along with the arms were the usual things that people of the Southwest buried with their honored dead. Here lay three beautiful necklaces—for a person who had no neck; a pipe to be smoked, at some pleasant ceremony in the afterworld, by a man who had no lips to puff with; and handsome sandals for this footless one to wear as he journeyed to the place where he would meet the spirits of his ancestors.

The Morrises rubbed their eyes and looked again to be sure the grave had not been opened and the rest of the body removed. Not a chance. The hole had been made exactly to fit the contents. Could it be that some huge piece of rock fell from the canyon wall near by and trapped a man, leaving only his hands and arms for others to find and bury? Probably no one will ever know.

Where Did It Come From?

Did the Indians of Central America think up all their own ideas and inventions, or were some things borrowed from far-off Asia? There are pyramids in one part of Asia almost exactly like those in Central America. In another part of Asia, people made religious books on just the same kind of paper, folded in the same accordion shape as the Aztec and Mayan books. The Aztecs played a game that is very much like parcheesi, which comes from India.

Ancient Asians had boats that could carry them long distances. Did some of them sail across the Pacific, bringing ideas which sprouted and spread in the Americas? Some scholars say, "Yes." Others say definitely, "No!"

When? Where? How?

Other missing stories can perhaps be told when archeologists finally discover enough facts. Here are some of the most important ones:

How did early Americans learn to make pottery? Did someone bring the knowledge from Asia? Or was pottery invented here? Was it invented several different times in the Americas? If so, when and where?

Where did corn come from? Experts agree that farmers developed corn from some wild plant, but which one? When?

For that matter, where did the ancestors of the Indians, themselves, live? Maybe if you become an archeologist you can find out.

PROBLEMATICALS

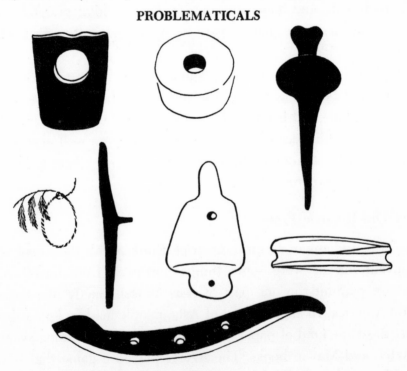

Indians made these objects. If you can figure out what they were used for, you know more than the archeologists know.

10

Archeology and You

When Frank Cushing was nine years old, he went out one day to watch his father's hired man plowing a field. The man showed Frank something he had picked from the freshly turned earth. "It's an arrowhead," he said. "The Indians made it."

The cold, shiny, sharp little piece of flint fascinated Frank. From then on he spent every spare minute looking for Indian relics, and there were many to be found in western New York where he lived. By the time he was fourteen, he had a collection of several hundred Indian things. When summer came he pitched a tent, and camped at a place where the digging was good.

As Frank dug and collected, he wondered. How did the Indians make all their flint and obsidian knives and arrowheads? No one in all of western New York was able to tell him. As a matter of fact, no archeologist in the world could answer the question that young Frank Cushing was asking in the summer of 1871. If he wanted to know, he had to find out for himself, and that is just what he proceeded to do.

Since glass seemed very much like flint and obsidian, he experimented with broken bottles and chunks of plate glass. He hammered and tapped, and in time he managed to shape things that looked like arrowheads. But his glass arrowheads were not nearly so good as the real Indian ones, and he knew it, though he could not figure out why.

Frank decided to try something else. He found an Indian harpoon made of bone and started to copy it. Since he did not have any fresh bone handy, he used the next best thing—the handle of his toothbrush. He wanted to use only the kind of tools Indians had, and he set to work with chips of flint. These worked beautifully so long as he moved a sharp edge back and forth with a sawing motion. But when he tried to use a piece of flint for scraping he had trouble. Flakes of the flint kept snapping off. The soft toothbrush handle was breaking the hard flint!

This gave Frank an idea. Maybe he could shape flint tools by *pressing* off flakes with the toothbrush handle. Soon he was making much better arrowheads than he ever managed to do by hammering and tapping. He had discovered an Indian secret!

Now he was even more interested than before. He kept on digging and collecting, and learned so much that he finally was able to find work as an Indian expert. His whole life was devoted to a study which began when he was a nine-year-old boy holding his first arrowheads.

This same kind of thing has happened to other boys and girls, too. When Julio Tello was ten years old, he had a chance to look at some remarkable skulls that came from ancient graves in Peru. These skulls had neat little holes in them, as if someone had cut through the bone on purpose. Indeed someone had. Skilled Indian doctors, long ago, performed amazing operations, using sharp stone tools. Did they give some sort of anesthetic when they operated? The Indians of Peru knew about one pain-killing drug at least. Maybe, they also knew how to hypnotize patients and make them forget pain.

Young Julio Tello examined the skulls with wonder and excitement and pride. He, himself, was a Peruvian Indian. Had one of those Indian surgeons been an ancestor of his? At any rate, he determined to learn more about the early inhabitants of his country, and he succeeded. He became a famous archeologist, a discoverer of many things about the different peoples who lived in Peru.

The Youngest Archeologist

Earl Morris was three and a half years old when he excavated a prehistoric grave for the first time. His family lived in a log cabin near one of the ruins in New Mexico, and his father often dug up the pottery and tools that vanished people had left behind. Of course, Earl wanted to help. So he was given a short-handled pick of his own. One whack

132

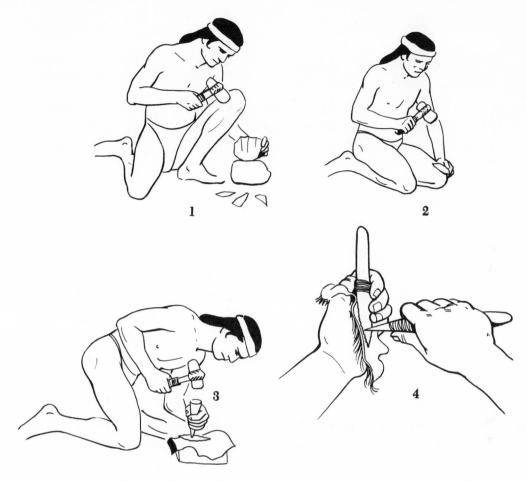

(1) To make a flint arrowhead or knife blade, an Indian first broke a lump of flint—a kind of stone that is very hard but very brittle. The right kind of blow with his stone hammer made the flint split off in large flakes. (2) Next he trimmed the flake and shaped it by tapping it lightly around the edges with a hammer, (3) or by tapping it with a hammer and a punch made of deer antler or bone. (4) He did the final delicate trimming and sharpening by pressure—not by pounding or tapping. In one hand he held the flint on a pad to protect the palm from cuts. In the other hand he held a tool made of antler or bone. With the tool he pressed down again and again, all around the edge of the flint. This pressure on the *upper* side made tiny flakes snap off the *under* side. A skillful flint worker could finish an arrowhead in less than fifteen minutes.

WARNING: Wear safety goggles when you try to make your own arrowheads. A tiny flake can snap into your eye and do great damage.

at the earth uncovered a beautiful white and black dipper. His excitement brought his mother running with a kitchen knife still in her hand. Together they loosened the dipper, then with pick and knife

133

dug on and discovered the skeleton of the Old One with whom the pot had been buried.

From that moment, Earl Morris never doubted what he wanted to do. When he was sixty-three years old and a famous authority on Indian Americans, he liked to say that he had been an archeologist for sixty years.

Hurry, Hurry!

It was easy for anybody to go out and dig and find things when Frank Cushing was young. Nobody cared how much a young fellow poked around looking for Indian relics. There was no real science of archeology then. Men like Cushing helped to make it. The more they learned about digging, the more they regretted the way they dug when they first started. Even the most careful threw away things that later proved to be valuable. Who could have guessed that charcoal ought to be saved because invisible atomic clocks were ticking away in it?

Nowadays, the United States has fewer and fewer places to dig. Scientists want to find out all they possibly can in every one of these spots. That is why they ask people not to dig without expert advice. This does not mean that they want to discourage anyone who is interested in the secrets that the earth still holds. Far from it. Archeologists actually need everybody's help. They have a tremendous amount of digging to do right away in many places. If they do not dig now it will be too late.

It may seem hard to believe that ruins or campsites which have lasted for hundreds of years will suddenly disappear before our eyes, but just that is happening in the United States. Indians made their homes and camps near water, often along streams and rivers. A great many rivers are now being dammed up, and behind every dam an artificial lake will rise.

This vast dam-building program was started by the United States government in 1945. When archeologists heard about it, they were filled with dismay. They realized that water would soon cover eighty per cent of all known sites where ancient Americans once lived. Men

134

Skin diving off the coast of California, boys found dozens of stone bowls which experts have not yet explained.

with shovels and trowels had to begin a race against the bulldozers of construction crews. Fortunately the engineers did not start all the dams at once. By working fast, the archeologists could examine the most important sites. They dug like gophers. In five years they saved from the rising water more than four million separate bits of evidence about ancient man.

This now-or-never digging is called "salvage archeology," and in many places volunteers help with it. For example, a former Mayor of Platte, South Dakota, gathered a crew of old men who had retired from their jobs. A plasterer, a restaurant manager, an oil-well driller, and others excavated a site on the bank of the Missouri River. The place turned out to be a village built by the Arikara (ah-REE-kah-rah) Indians about 250 years ago. The old men were so enthusiastic that they dug on. Beneath this village they discovered another one four hundred years older. Experts all agreed that these amateurs did a beautiful piece of work.

Discoveries were also made along other rivers far out in the center of the Great Plains. The experts already knew a good deal about the ancient people who lived in forests along the edge of the prairies, but now suddenly they began to get fascinating information about Indians who were farmers—not buffalo hunters—in the very heart of the flat grassy lands.

These early Plains Indians made their homes in lodges—houses partly sunk in the ground and roofed over with logs covered with earth. The earth-lodge people were village dwellers, stay-at-homes. Then Spanish horses came onto the Plains, and horses changed everything. Settled farmers became wandering hunters. They left their solid earth lodges and began to live in skin tepees that could be easily moved from place to place. Archeologists are finding new chapters in this story— and many others—as they dig along the river banks ahead of rising new lakes.

Trowels are also racing bulldozers in some of the places where natural gas companies bury their long-distance pipelines. In one such contest, archeologists walked every inch of the way between New Mexico and the state of Washington — walked it not once but twice. Four teams of scientists went on foot ahead of the ditch-digging equipment, scouting for sites. They covered 1500 miles along the main pipeline and another 1500 miles along branch lines, and they saw a great deal that interested them.

With the help of workmen they excavated the most important sites. Then, after the ditch was dug, they made their second trip over the entire 3000 miles. This time they studied the walls of the empty ditch, looking for signs of prehistoric man that did not appear on the surface. On this second trip they made more discoveries. Altogether, in the 3000 mile ribbon of earth, they found 122 sites that no one had ever seen before — and no one would ever have a chance to see again.

This same kind of now-or-never digging goes on ahead of many road-building and construction crews. Often the archeologists directing salvage operations need and welcome help. If you want to lend a hand, write to the archeological society nearest to your home. You will find it listed in the back of this book.

1   I   •

Your Eyes Can Help

What if you can not always go where the archeologists need you, when they need you? You can still help — with your eyes.

Suppose you go hiking and find chips of flint under a sheltering ledge or bits of pottery sticking out of the soil in a field. Or possibly — just possibly — you might see some bones uncovered where men are digging the foundation for a new building. What would you do?

Would you get busy with a shovel or trowel and start digging, too? Many people have done just that, and they have destroyed priceless information. We would know a great deal more than we do about the Old Ones at Mesa Verde if pot hunters and souvenir collectors had not looted the place before scientists could get there. People have found very ancient fluted points in many parts of New York and Pennsylvania and other states in the east. But the value of these discoveries was completely lost because sharp eyes did not often go with keen memory. Collectors took the fossils home and could not tell archeologists *exactly* where they had come from.

Pot hunters in Mexico and Peru and other places still rob ancient graves and sell what they find to tourists and curio collectors, although their countries have laws against this. The United States has such a law, too. It is called the Antiquities Act. It is designed to save all that is left of our Indian heritage, so that scientists can study it, and everybody can enjoy it — not just those who happen to get there first.

Does this law mean that you can not ever dig or collect? Not at all. A great deal of digging goes on all the time, and it is done by amateurs. But they have the guidance of experts who make sure they get the best possible results. And they have permission from the government or from the private individuals who own the land on which they dig.

Do's and Don'ts for Amateurs

If you want to take part in the fascinating search for Indian relics and for clues to ancient mysteries, you can have fun and do a good job at the same time by following these rules:

1. *Look and learn, don't loot!*
2. *Report anything you find* to the nearest archeological society or museum.
3. *Never dig* without permission and expert guidance. The nearest archeological society will tell you how to get permission and advice.
4. *Don't touch, don't move* any of the following things, until you have consulted an archeologist: fluted points, bannerstones, birdstones, anything made of polished slate, plummets, burials, corncobs (in the Southwest), pottery.

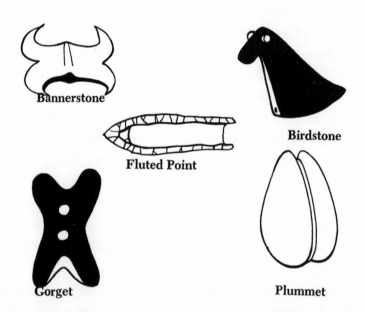

Bannerstone

Fluted Point

Birdstone

Gorget

Plummet

5. *Volunteer to help* the nearest archeological society. There is plenty of work for careful amateurs to do.

Why these rules?

No matter how careful an inexperienced person is, he may destroy evidence that an expert needs. The *exact* position of a spear point in the earth may tell a fascinating chapter in human history. If that position is changed, ever so little, the story may vanish — forever.

When you see an archeologist dig, you will notice first of all how careful he is. There is a good reason for this. He can never correct a mistake he has made in digging. He gets no second chance. Once he has dug up something, he can never dig that same thing up again. All he can do is avoid the same kind of mistake the next time.

Fortunately there is still a great deal to dig up. In the Southwest and in Central and South America and in the Far North it will be a long time before archeologists work themselves out of a job. In our part of the world, as well as in the rest of it, there are still great mysteries to be solved. What were ancient people really like? How did they live and love and die during the 500,000 years before they invented writing?

Historians can study what men have written down. But writing began only 5,000 years ago, and it was slow in spreading. It has not reached some places even today. Historians can not tell us anything about the millions and billions of people who left us no written stories of their lives. This is the job of the archeologists who dig in the earth.

But archeology can be much more than detective work. If you look with the right kind of eye at a spear point made of stone, you can see the man who shaped it. You may even get a glimpse of the giant bison or the lumbering mastodon he hunted. In a broken piece of pottery you can see a whole cooking vessel. A second look will reveal the woman who made that pot. You may even see her cooking corn meal mush or grinding corn or growing it in the earth.

In a bit of bone and string you may see a child's toy and the boys and girls who played with it. You may see the keen dark eyes of those children as they laughed and tried out new things and learned.

In *things* you can see *people* — that's archeology.

11

More About Archeology

Archeological Sites, Museums, Organizations

Material is arranged by state in this order: (1) archeological societies or other groups concerned with archeology (for addresses of local chapters of state societies, apply to the state organization); (2) museums that have interesting collections of archeological material; (3) Indian archeological sites that are open to the public. When museums are attached to these, the fact is noted in italics.

NATIONAL ORGANIZATIONS

Archeological Institute of America
Andover Hall
Cambridge, Mass.
(Publishes *Archeology Magazine*)

Society for American Archeology
University Museums Bldg.
Ann Arbor, Mich.
(Publishes *American Antiquity*)

ALABAMA

Alabama Museum of Natural History
University of Alabama
University

Mound State Monument
Moundville
mounds, museum

ALASKA

Alaska Historical Library and Museum
Box 2051, Juneau

ARIZONA

Ariz. Archeological and Historical Society
State Museum
Tucson

Yavapai County Archeological Society
Box 937, Prescott

Amerind Foundations
Dragoon
museum

Heard Museum
22 E. Monte Vista Rd.
Phoenix

Museum of Northern Arizona
Flagstaff

Petrified Forest National Monument Museum
Near Holbrook, off US 66

Southwestern Monuments Assn.
Box 1562, Globe
museum

Wayside Museum of Archeology
Grand Canyon National Park

Canyon de Chelly National Monument
Navaho Indian Reservation
cliff dwellings

Casa Grande National Monument
Near Coolidge, on State 87
tower, ruins, museum

Kinishba Pueblo
Near Fort Apache, off State 73
partly restored ruins

Montezuma Castle National Monument
Near Camp Verde, off US 89A
five-story cliff dwelling

Navajo National Monument
Navajo Indian Reservation
the Betatakin and Keet Seel cliff dwellings

Pueblo Grande City Park
Phoenix
a Hohokam ruin, museum

Tonto National Monument
Near Roosevelt, on State 88
cliff dwellings, museum

Tuzigoot National Monument
Near Clarkdale, off US 89A
pueblo ruins, museum

Walnut Canyon National Monument
Near Flagstaff, off US 66
cliff dwellings, museum

Wupatki National Monument
Off US 89, 45 miles from Flagstaff
ruins, ancient ball court

ARKANSAS

Arkansas Archeological Society
Univ. of Arkansas Museum
Fayetteville

CALIFORNIA

Southwestern Anthropological Association
c/o S. L. Rogers, San Diego State College
San Diego

Antelope Valley Indian Research Museum
Wilsona Route, Lancaster

Los Angeles County Museum
Exposition Park
Los Angeles

Museum of Anthropology
Univ. of California
Berkeley

Indian Museum
Lakeport

Oakland Public Museum
1426 Oak St.
Oakland

140

Municipal Museum
Riverside

San Diego Museum of Man
Balboa Park, San Diego

Calif. Academy of Sciences
San Francisco

Museum of Natural History
Santa Barbara

Southwest Museum
Highland Park, Los Angeles

State Indian Museum
2618 K St., Sacramento

Clear Lake State Park
Near Kelseyville
Lake County
*Pomo sweat houses and
ceremonial houses are
being restored. Other
State Parks contain
many sites. See rangers
for locations.*

COLORADO

Colorado Archeological
Society
Univ. of Colorado
Boulder

Denver Art Museum
1300 Logan St., Denver

Denver Museum of
Natural History
City Park, Denver

Colo. State Museum
Denver

Fine Arts Center
Colorado Springs
museum

Univ. of Colo. Museum
Boulder

Mesa Verde National Park
Between Mancos and Cortez,
off US 160
*cliff dwellings, basket maker
houses, guides, lectures,
museum*

Hovenweep National Monument
Near Mesa Verde
Anasazi ruins

CONNECTICUT

Archeological Society
of Connecticut
c/o Frank Glynn
37 High St., Clinton

Peabody Museum
Yale University
New Haven

DELAWARE

Archeological Society of
Delaware
15 Myrtle Ave., Claymont

Hagley Museum
Wilmington

Delaware State Museum
Dover

Zwaanendael Museum
Lewes

FLORIDA

Broward County
Archeological Society
Box 2003, Hollywood

Florida Anthropological
Society

Florida State Museum
Gainesville

University Museum
Florida State Univ.
Tallahassee

GEORGIA

Society for Preservation
of Early Ga. History
Dept. of Archeology
Univ. of Georgia
Athens

Northwest Georgia
Archeological Society
c/o L. Lipps
Shorter College
Rome

Southeastern Archeological
Conference
Ocmulgee National
Monument
Macon

Etowah Mounds
Cartersville
*temple, burial mounds,
museum*

Kolomoki Mounds State
Park
Near Blakely, on US 27
*temple, burial mounds,
museum*

Ocmulgee National
Monument
Macon
*temple mound, underground
lodge, museum*

IDAHO

Idaho State College Museum
Pocatello

ILLINOIS

State Archeological Society
Southern Illinois University
Museum
Carbondale

Chicago Natural History
Museum
Chicago

Illinois State Museum
Springfield

Museum of Natural Hist.
Univ. of Illinois
Urbana

Dickson Mounds State
Memorial

Near Havana and
Lewistown, off State 78
skeletons in burial mound

Cahokia Mounds State Park
East St. Louis, on State 3
*largest temple mound;
other mounds exist in
or near these State Parks:
Mississippi Palisades, Pere
Marquette, Starved Rock,
Buffalo Rock*

INDIANA

Indiana Historical Society
140 North Senate Ave.
Indianapolis

Indiana State Museum
Indianapolis

IOWA

Iowa Archeological Society
c/o Mrs. A. I. Mason
2307 B Ave., Cedar Rapids

Archeology Dept.
State Univ.
Iowa City

Davenport Public Museum
Davenport

Museum of Natural Hist.
State University
Iowa City

Effigy Mounds National
Monument
Near Marquette, State 13
mounds in animal shapes

KANSAS

Natural History Museum
University of Kansas
Lawrence

KENTUCKY

Museum of Anthropology
Univ. of Kentucky
Lexington

Adena Park
Near Lexington, off US 27
and 68
*mound; for permission to
visit, apply to
Univ. of Ky.*

Ancient Buried City
Near Wickliffe, on US 51
*temple and burial mounds;
private, admission fee*

Central Park
Ashland
burial mounds

Mammoth Cave National
Park
Near Cave City, off State 70
museum

LOUISIANA

Middle American Research
Institute
Tulane University
New Orleans
museum

141

Louisiana State Exhibit
  Museum
Shreveport
Louisiana State Museum
New Orleans
Marksville State Monument
Near Marksville, off State 1
*temple and burial mounds;
  museum*

Poverty Point
East of Epps, on Bayou
  Macon
*geometric mounds, on
  private property; no
  entrance fee*

MAINE
The Archeological Society
Robert Abbe Museum of
  Stone Age Antiquities
Bar Harbor

Wilson Museum
Castine

MARYLAND
Archeological Society of
  Maryland
c/o Mr. T. L. Ford
1906 Ruxton Rd.
Ruxton

MASSACHUSETTS
Archeological Institute
  of America
Andover Hall
Cambridge

Mass. Archeological
  Society
Bronson Museum
Attleboro

Peabody Museum
Harvard University
Cambridge

Peabody Museum of Salem
Salem

Robert S. Peabody Founda-
  tion for Archeology
Phillips Academy
Andover

Dighton Rock State Park
Near Berkley
*carvings on Dighton Rock
  have been subject of much
  disagreement*

MICHIGAN
Michigan Archeological
  Society
c/o George Davis
501 Comstock Road, N.E.
Grand Rapids

Cranbrook Institute of
  Science
Bloomfield Hills

Kelsey Museum of
  Archeology
Univ. of Michigan
Ann Arbor

MINNESOTA
Minnesota Archeological
  Society

Minneapolis Public Library
Minneapolis
museum

Minnesota Historical Society
Cedar and Central Streets
St. Paul
museum

Pipestone National
  Monument
Near Pipestone, off US 75
ancient quarries

MISSISSIPPI
Univ. of Miss. Museum
University

MISSOURI
Missouri Archeological
  Society
15 Switzler Hall
Univ. of Missouri
Columbia

Missouri Resources Museum
State Capitol Bldg.
Jefferson City

Museum of Science
Academy of Science
St. Louis

Kansas City Museum
3218 Gladstone Blvd.
Kansas City

St. Joseph Museum
310 South 11 Street
St. Joseph

Van Meter State Park
Near Marshall, off
  State 122
Hopewellian mounds

Washington State Park
Near DeSoto, on State 21
*prehistoric Indian
  rock carvings*

MONTANA
Historical Society of
  Montana
State Historical Museum
Helena

Montana State College
  Museum
Bozeman

Montana State University
  Museum
Missoula

Museum of the Plains
  Indian
Browning

Pictographs (carvings on
  rock) fenced off and
  protected along US 2
  west of Kalispel

NEBRASKA
Laboratory of Anthropology
Univ. of Nebraska
Lincoln

Nebraska State Historical
  Society
1500 R. Street
Lincoln
museum

Univ. of Nebraska Museum
Lincoln
NEVADA
Nevada State Museum
Carson City

NEW HAMPSHIRE
New Hampshire
  Archeological Society
c/o Col. G. L. Prindle
Great Bay Rd.
Greenland

NEW JERSEY
Archeological Society of
  New Jersey
c/o Mrs. K. B. Greywacz
State Museum, Trenton

Archeological Laboratory
Dr. Dorothy Cross, State
  Archeologist
State House Annex
Trenton

Newark Museum
49 Washington St.
Newark

New Jersey State Museum
State House Annex
Trenton

NEW MEXICO
Archeological Society of
  New Mexico
Museum of New Mexico
Santa Fe

Grant County Archaeological
  Society
Silver City

Grant County Archaeological
  Museum
Silver City

Laboratory of Anthropology
  Museum
Santa Fe

Roosevelt County Museum
Portales

Museum of Anthropology
Univ. of New Mexico
Albuquerque

Museum of New Mexico
Santa Fe

Abo State Monument
Near Mountainair,
  off US 60
large Pueblo ruin

Aztec Ruins National
  Monument
Aztec, on US 550
*large ruin; very large kiva;
  museum*

Bandelier National
  Monument
45 mi. west of Santa Fe,
  off State 4
*4 ruins; 300 hand-hewn
  caves; museum*

Chaco Canyon National
  Monument
64 mi. north of Thoreau,
  on State 56

142

18 big ruins, including
  Pueblo Bonito; museum

Coronado State Monument
near Bernalillo on US 85
ruins; museum

Folsom State Monument
Near Folsom, off US 64
site of discovery of
  first Folsom point

Gila Cliff Dwelling National
  Monument
No auto road; write to
  custodian, Box 101
Silver City
cliff dwellings

Gran Quivira National
  Monument
25 mi. south of Mountainair,
  on State 10
large ruin

Jemez State Monument
Near Jemez Springs,
  on State 4
ancient pueblo

Pecos State Monument
Near Pecos, off US 84
ruins of large pueblo

Quarai State Monument
Near Mountainair,
  off State 10
large ruin

NEW YORK
New York State
  Archeological Assn.
c/o Dr. Marian E. White
Buffalo Museum of Science
Humboldt Park
Buffalo

Rochester Museum of Arts
  and Sciences
657 East Ave.
Rochester

Museum of the American
  Indian, Heye Foundation
Broadway and 155 St.
New York

Brooklyn Museum
Washington Ave. and
  Eastern Parkway
Brooklyn

American Museum of
  Natural History
79 Street and Central
  Park West, New York

Museum of Primitive Art
15 West 54 St., New York

New York State Museum
State Education Bldg.
Albany

NORTH CAROLINA
Archeological Society of
  North Carolina
c/o Mr. J. L. Coe
Box 561, Chapel Hill

Laboratory of Anthropology
Univ. of North Carolina
Chapel Hill

Town Creek Indian Mound
Mt. Gilead, on State 73
temple mound,
  reconstructed temple,
  museum

NORTH DAKOTA
State Historical Society of
  North Dakota
Liberty Memorial Bldg.
Bismarck
museum

Crowley Flint Quarry
17 mi. north of Hebron,
  off US 10
quarry where Indians got
  flint for arrowheads

Double Ditch Indian Site
12 mi. north of Bismarck
  on east bank of Missouri
  River
ruins of Mandan village

Ft. Clark Historic Site
Near Ft. Clark, southeast
  of Stanton on State 25
Mandan and Arikara
  village

Huff Indian Village
1 mi. south of Huff
ruins of Mandan village

Menoken Indian Village
  Historic Site
1¼ mi. north of Menoken,
  off US 10
ruins of Mandan village

Molander Indian Village
3 mi. north of Price, on
  west bank of Missouri
earth lodge village

Ft. Lincoln State Park
near Mandan, off US 10
reconstructed earth
  lodges; museum

OHIO
Ohio Historical Society
Ohio State Museum
Columbus 10

Campbell Mound
On McKinley Ave.
Columbus
burial mound

Flint Ridge
2 mi. north of Brownsville,
  on State 668
prehistoric Indian flint
  quarry

Fort Ancient
7 mi. southeast of Lebanon,
  on State 350
earthworks, museum

Fort Hill State Memorial
18 mi. southeast of Hillsboro
  off State 41 and 124
Hopewellian earthworks

Leo Petroglyph
4 mi. northwest of Coalton,
  off US 35
Indian pictographs on rock

Miamisburg Mound
1 mi. southeast of Miamisburg, on US 25
large conical burial mound

Mound City Group National
  Monument
Near Chillicothe on State
  104
Hopewellian mounds,
  museum

Newark Earthworks
3 sites in the city of
  Newark: Octagon State
  Memorial (North 33
  Street); Wright Earth-
  works (James and Waldo
  Streets); Mound Builders
  State Memorial (on
  State 79)
geometrical Hopewell
  mounds

Seip Mound
3 mi. east of Bainbridge on
  US 50
burial mound

Serpent Mound
4 mi. northwest of Locust
  Grove on State 73
large effigy mound

Story Mound
Delano Ave., 1 block south
  of Allen Ave.
Chillicothe
conical Adena mound

Tarlton Cross Mound
1 mi. north of Tarlton,
  off State 159
effigy mound

Warren County Serpent
  Mound
Near Rochester, on US 22
effigy mound

OKLAHOMA
Oklahoma Anthropological
  Society
Univ. of Oklahoma
Norman

Southern Plains Indian
  Museum
Anadarko

Philbrook Art Center
Tulsa
museum

Stovall Museum of Science
  and History
Univ. of Oklahoma
Norman

OREGON
Museum of Natural History
Univ. of Oregon
Eugene

Portland Art Museum
Portland

PENNSYLVANIA
Society for Pennsylvania
  Archeology
c/o V. R. Mrozoski
407 Phillips St., Aliquippa

University Museum
33 and Spruce Streets
Philadelphia

Carnegie Museum
4400 Forbes St.
Pittsburgh

State Museum
Harrisburg

Reading Public Museum and
Art Gallery
Museum Rd. and Parkside
Dr., Reading

RHODE ISLAND
Narragansett Archeo-
logical Society of
Rhode Island
c/o Edward D. Cook
Box 154
Hundred Acre Pond Rd.
West Kingston

Haffenreffer Museum of
the American Indian
Brown University
Providence

Great Swamp Fight Site
35 mi. south of Providence,
on State 2, 1 mi. east of
road
*last stand of Indians in
King Phillip's War*

Indian Burial Grounds
39 mi. south of Providence
on State 2, 1 mi. north
of Cross Mills

SOUTH DAKOTA
South Dakota Historical
Society
Soldiers Memorial
Pierre

W. H. Over Museum
Univ. of South Dakota
Vermillion

TENNESSEE
Dept. of Anthropology
Univ. of Tennessee
Knoxville

Chucalissa Indian Museum
1987 Indian Village Dr.
Memphis
*burial mound, temple
mound, some buildings
restored*

TEXAS
Texas Archeological and
Paleontological Society
Abilene

Texas Archeological
Society
Dept. of Anthropology
Univ. of Texas
Austin

Central Texas Archeological
Society
Box 1176, c/o F. H. Watt
Waco

West Texas Historical and
Scientific Society
906 East Ave. D
Alpine
museum

Witte Memorial Museum
Brackenridge Park
San Antonio

UTAH
University Archeological
Society
Brigham Young Univ.
Provo

Utah Statewide Archeo-
logical Society
Univ. of Utah
Salt Lake City

Utah Museum of Fine Arts
Univ. of Utah
Salt Lake City

VIRGINIA
Archeological Society of
Virginia
c/o Mrs. G. A. Robertson
3718 Brookside Rd.
Richmond

WASHINGTON
Washington State Museum
Univ. of Washington
Seattle

Eastern Wash. State
Historical Society
West 2316 First Ave.
Spokane
museum

Indian rock paintings
Near Yakima on US 410;
also on Little Spokane
River above junction
with Spokane River

Sacajawea Museum
Sacajawea State Park
South of Pasco on US 395

Old Man House
East of Poulsbo, on
Bainbridge Island

WASHINGTON D.C.
Smithsonian Institution
Washington, D. C.
museum

WEST VIRGINIA
West Virginia Archeological
Society
c/o Charles J. Lally
314 Garfield St.
McMecham

Grave Creek Mound (or
Mammoth Mound)
Tomlinson Ave., between
9th and 10th Streets
Moundsville
*very large conical mound,
Adena culture; museum*

WISCONSIN
State Historical Society
816 State St.
Madison
museum

Wisconsin Archeological
Society
c/o Milwaukee Public
Museum
Milwaukee

Logan Museum of
Anthropology
Beloit College
Beloit

Neville Public Museum
Green Bay

Milwaukee Public Museum
818 West Wisconsin Ave.
Milwaukee

Aztalan State Park
Between Lakemills and
Johnson Creek, off
State 30
*temple mound, village,
partly rebuilt*

Lizard Mound State Park
Near West Bend, off
State 144, on County A
31 effigy mounds

WYOMING
Dept. of Anthropology
Univ. of Wyoming
Laramie

State Museum
Cheyenne

CANADA
Archeological Association
of Quebec
c/o Ian Clark
3571 Shuter St., Montreal

Ontario Archeological
Society
c/o Ogden Hershaw
38 Farnham Ave., Toronto

McGill Univ. Museum
Montreal

Montreal Museum of Fine
Arts
1379 Sherbrooke St., W.
Montreal

Museums of Geology,
Archeology and Ethnology
Univ. of Alberta
Edmonton

National Museum of Canada
Ottowa

Royal Ontario Museum
Queens Park, Toronto

Provincial Museum of
Saskatchewan
Saskatoon

Museum of Anthropology
Univ. of British Columbia
Vancouver

Vancouver City Museum
Vancouver

Provincial Museum of
Natural History and
Anthropology
Parliament Bldg.
Victoria

12 Books, Magazines

For Young People–the Americas

AMERICANS BEFORE COLUMBUS
by Elizabeth Baity (Viking, 1951)

THE FIRST BOOK OF INDIANS
by Benjamin Brewster [Franklin Folsom]
(Watts, 1950)

BUFFALO KILL by Gardell D. Christensen
(Nelson, 1959)
*How Plains Indians hunted buffalo before
the coming of horses*

THE AMERICAN INDIAN by Sydney E.
Fletcher (Grosset & Dunlap, 1954)

INDIANS OF THE FOUR CORNERS
by Alice Lee Marriott (Crowell, 1952)
Ancient people in the Southwest

DIGGING IN THE SOUTHWEST by Ann
Axtell Morris (Doubleday, 1933)
Personal stories of excavations

DIGGING IN YUCATAN by Ann Axtell
Morris (Doubleday, 1931)
More stories of excavations

DEREK IN MESA VERDE by Derek
Nussbaum (Putnam, 1926)
*Autobiographical story of a boy who helped
with excavation of cliff dwellings*

BOOK OF INDIAN LIFE CRAFTS
by Oscar E. Norbeck (Association Press,
1958)
*Instructions for making many things as
the Indians made them*

THE INDIAN HOW BOOK by Arthur C.
Parker (Doran, 1927)
How Indians did many things

SUN KINGDOM OF THE AZTECS
by Victor W. von Hagen (World, 1958)

PREHISTORIC AMERICA by Anne Terry
White (Random House, 1951)
*First half about animals, second half
about people*

—The World

THE FIRST PEOPLE IN THE WORLD
by Gerald Ames and Rose Wyler
(Harper, 1958)

DIGGING INTO YESTERDAY by Estelle
Friedman (Putnam, 1958)

EVERYDAY LIFE IN PREHISTORIC
TIMES by Marjorie and C. H. B. Quennell
(Putnam, 1959)

HOW THE FIRST MEN LIVED
by Lancelot Hogben (Lothrop, 1952)

SECRETS IN THE DUST by Raymond
Holden (Dodd Mead, 1959)

THE WONDERFUL WORLD OF
ARCHEOLOGY by Ronald Jessup
(Doubleday, 1956)

THE FIRST BOOK OF ARCHEOLOGY
by Nora Kubie (Watts, 1957)

MAN'S WAY FROM CAVE TO
SKYSCRAPER by Ralph and Adelin Linton
(Harper, 1947)

ALL ABOUT ARCHEOLOGY by Anne
Terry White (Random House, 1959)

THE FIRST MEN IN THE WORLD
by Anne Terry White (Random House,
1953)

LOST WORLDS: THE ROMANCE OF
ARCHEOLOGY by Anne Terry White
(Random House, 1941)

For the Whole Family

LOST CITY OF THE INCAS by Hiram
Bingham (Duell, Sloan & Pearce, 1948)
Autobiographical story of discovery

GODS, GRAVES, AND SCHOLARS
by C. W. Ceram (Knopf, 1951)
Stories of famous discoveries

THE MARCH OF ARCHEOLOGY
by C. W. Ceram (Knopf, 1958)
A pictorial history

THE EAGLE, THE JAGUAR, AND THE
SERPENT by Miguel Covarrubias
(Knopf, 1954)
Indian art of Alaska, Canada and U. S.

INDIAN ART OF MEXICO AND
CENTRAL AMERICA by Miguel
Covarrubias (Knopf, 1957)

SUN CIRCLES AND HUMAN HANDS
edited by Emma Lila Fundaburk and
Mary Douglass Foreman (Fundaburk,
Luverne, Ala., 1957)
Southeastern Indians—many pictures

PICTORIAL HISTORY OF THE
AMERICAN INDIAN by Oliver
LaFarge (Crown, 1956)

TRIBES THAT SLUMBER by Thomas
M. N. Lewis and Madeline Kneberg
(Univ. of Tennessee Press, 1958)
*People of the Tennessee area, including
mound builders*

RICHARD WETHERILL: ANASAZI
by Frank McNitt (Univ. of New Mexico
Press, 1957)
*Biography of the cowboy who explored the
Anasazi ruins*

THE CIVILIZATION OF THE MAYAS
by J. Eric S. Thompson (Chicago
Natural History Museum, 1958)

PEOPLE OF THE SERPENT by Edward
H. Thompson (Houghton Mifflin, 1932)
Personal history of digging in Maya land

For Parents and Teachers

PREHISTORIC MEN by Robert J. Braidwood (Chicago Natural History Museum, 1959)

NO STONE UNTURNED by Louis A. Brennan (Random House, 1959)
Provocative interpretation of North American archeology

PERU by Geoffrey H. S. Bushnell (Praeger, 1957)

A SHORT INTRODUCTION TO ARCHEOLOGY by V. Gordon Childe (Macmillan, 1958)

THE WORLD OF THE INCA by Bertrand Flornoy (Anchor, 1958)

A HISTORY OF THE ANCIENT SOUTHWEST by Harold S. Gladwin (Wheelwright, Portland, Maine, 1957)

THE ARCHEOLOGIST AT WORK by Robert F. Heizer (Harper, 1959)
Information on methods of digging; for professional archeologists but of interest also to amateurs

A MANUAL OF ARCHEOLOGICAL FIELD METHODS by Robert F. Heizer (National Press, Palo Alto, Calif., 1958)

TREASURE IN THE DUST by Frank C. Hibben (Lippincott, 1951)
Describes various prehistoric groups in the Americas

BACK OF HISTORY by William Howells (Doubleday, 1954)
The story of man to the beginning of written history

THE ORIGIN OF THINGS by Julius E. Lips (Premier)

DIGGING INTO HISTORY by Paul S. Martin (Chicago Natural History Museum, 1959)
Unearthing the Mogollon culture in New Mexico

THE ANCIENT CIVILIZATIONS OF PERU by J. Alden Mason (Pelican, 1957)

A MANUAL FOR NEANDERTHALS by H. Mewhinney (Univ. of Texas Press, 1957)
Detailed instructions for making arrowheads, spears, etc.

THE ANCIENT MAYA by S. G. Morley (Stanford Univ. Press, 1956)

THE TEMPLE OF THE WARRIORS by Earl H. Morris (Scribner, 1931)
The excavation of a Mayan temple

INCIDENTS OF TRAVEL IN CENTRAL AMERICA, CHIAPAS AND YUCATAN by John L. Stephens (Rutgers Univ. Press, 1957)
New edition of a book, published in 1841, by the first North American explorer of Mayan ruins

THE RISE AND FALL OF MAYA CIVILIZATION by J. Eric S. Thompson (Univ. of Oklahoma Press, 1956)

THE AZTECS OF MEXICO by George C. Vaillant (Pelican, 1950)

FREDERICK CATHERWOOD ARCHT. by Victor W. von Hagen (Oxford, 1950)
Biography of the first artist to visit Mayan ruins; illustrated with many of his drawings

HIGHWAY OF THE SUN by Victor W. von Hagen (Duell, Sloan & Pearce and Little Brown, 1955)
Exploration of the ancient Inca roads

REALM OF THE INCAS by Victor W. von Hagen (New American Library, 1957)

ARCHEOLOGY FROM THE EARTH by Mortimer Wheeler (Pelican, 1959)

ANCIENT MAN IN NORTH AMERICA by H. M. Wormington (Denver Museum of Natural History, (1957)

Magazines

American Antiquity

Archeology

Arizona Highways

Expedition

Natural History

The National Geographic

Films About Archeology

The following three films are available at the Archeological Institute of America, Andover Hall, Cambridge, Mass.

Betatakin. An ancient cliff dwelling in Arizona.

Point of Pines. How archeology students dig in a Pueblo ruin.

Tula to Tulum. An archeologist's adventures in Mexico.

The following may be obtained through your state museum or your state university film library. The name of the film's producer is given in parenthesis.

Ancient Earth. Archeologists at work, digging up ancient bones, tools and treasures, getting them ready to be exhibited in museums. (Univ. of Pennsylvania)

Aztecs. The story of the Aztec people of ancient Mexico. (Coronet)

Early American Civilizations. How Inca, Aztec and Mayan people lived long ago. (Coronet)

Glimpse of The Past. How archeologists put together the story of prehistoric American life. (Indiana Univ. Audio-Visual Center)

Heart of The Inca Empire. How the Incas may have built their great stone walls without machinery. Includes scenes at Machu Picchu. (Herbert Knapp for Coordinator of Inter-American Affairs)

Indians of Early America. How four different tribes of North American Indians lived in ancient times. (Encyclopaedia Britannica Films)

Jungle Quest for the Great Stone Heads. Archeologists at work on the mysteries of the Olmecs who carved gigantic heads of stone. (Coordinator of Inter-American Affairs)

Learning About the Past. How archeologists studied *things* that they found in an ancient mound-builder settlement and then figured out much about the *people* who once lived there. (Indiana Univ. Audio-Visual Center)

Maya of Ancient and Modern Yucatan. How Mayan Indians live today near the ruins of the great cities their ancestors built hundreds of years ago. (Guy D. Haselton)

Mayas. What the buildings, paintings, carvings, etc., found in Maya land tell about the people who lived there in ancient times. (Coronet)

Monuments of Ancient Mexico. Interesting discoveries in Mexico. This film was supervised by two famous archeologists. (George C. Vaillant and Kenneth Maggowan for Coordinator of Inter-American Affairs)

Story of Prehistoric Man. How ancient people made tools and weapons, learned about fire, invented farming; and how we know what happened so long ago. The scene is Europe, but the ideas are of general interest. (Coronet)

Tribe of the Turquoise Waters. Story of present-day Indians who live in the Grand Canyon and of the prehistoric people who were there first. (Avalon Daggett Prod.)

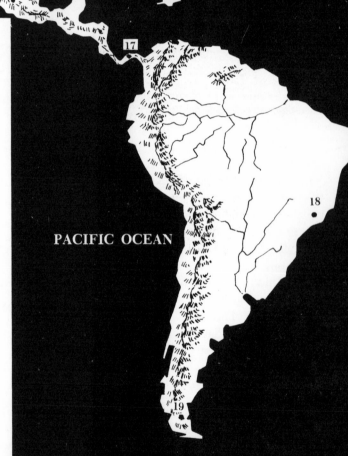

ATLANTIC OCEAN

PACIFIC OCEAN

THE VERY OLDEST AMERICANS

The numbers on the map show places where archeologists have discovered proof that people lived in America a very long time ago.

1 Angostura, South Dakota, about 9,400 years ago

2 Modoc Rock Shelter, Illinois, about 10,000 years ago

3 Lamoka Lake, New York, about 5,500 years ago

4 Bull Brook, Massachusetts, about 9,000 years ago

5 Melbourne, Florida, about 6,000 years ago

6 Russell Cave, Alabama, about 8,000 years ago

7 Fort Rock Cave, Oregon, about 9,000 years ago

8 Danger Cave, Utah, about 10,400 years ago

9 Santa Rosa Island, California, at least 27,000 years ago

10 Gypsum Cave, Nevada, about 10,000 years ago

11 Tule Springs, Nevada, about 23,800 years ago

12 Sandia Cave, New Mexico, estimated 15,000 years ago

13 Folsom, New Mexico, about 10,000 years ago

14 Clovis, New Mexico, estimated 13,000 years ago

15 Lewisville, Texas, at least 37,000 years ago

16 Tepexpan, Mexico, about 11,000 years ago

17 Cerro Mangote, Panama, about 6,800 years ago

18 Lagoa Santa, Brazil, between 5,000 and 10,000 years ago

19 Patagonia, Chile, about 8,500 years ago

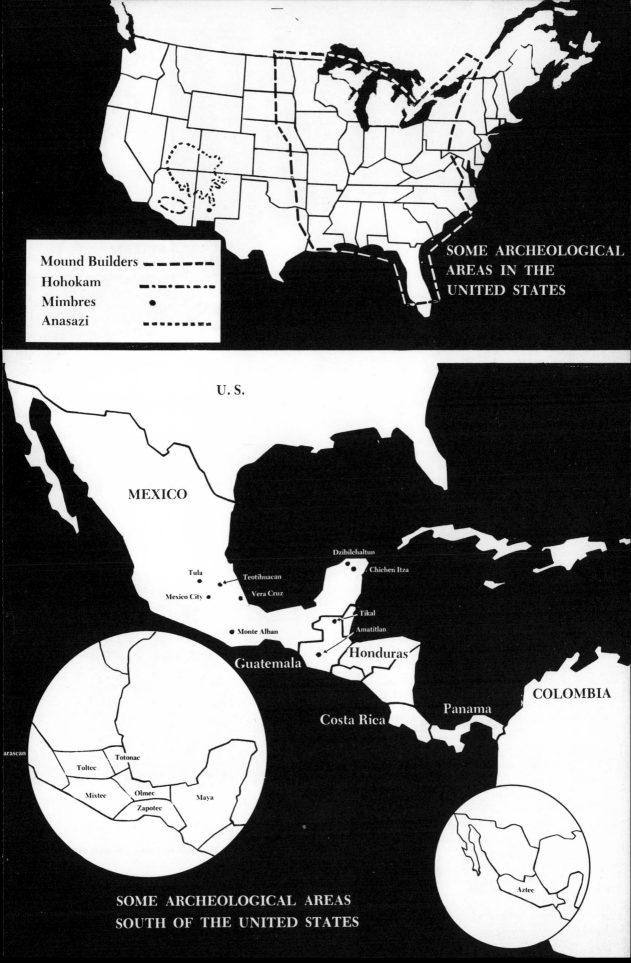

SOME ARCHEOLOGICAL AREAS IN THE UNITED STATES

Mound Builders ――――
Hohokam ―・―・―
Mimbres ●
Anasazi ━ ━ ━ ━

U. S.

MEXICO

Tula
Teotihuacan
Mexico City
Vera Cruz
Dzibilchaltun
Chichen Itza
Tikal
Amatitlan
Monte Alban
Honduras
Guatemala
COLOMBIA
Costa Rica
Panama

arascan
Toltec
Totonac
Mixtec
Olmec
Maya
Zapotec

Aztec

SOME ARCHEOLOGICAL AREAS SOUTH OF THE UNITED STATES

THE INCA
ROAD
SYSTEM

Quito

Talca

Amazon River

Chan-Chan

Quito

Viru Valley

Lima

Machu Picchu
Cuzco

Nazca

PERU

Lake Titicaca
Tiahuanaco

SOUTH AMERICA

PACIFIC OCEAN

CHILE

Talca

THE INCA EMPIRE AND IMPORTANT
PLACES IN PERU

Help and advice from many sources made this book possible. The authors owe a particular debt of gratitude to Dr. Dorothy Cross, New Jersey State Archeologist, who was ever generous with time and good suggestions. Special thanks go also to Dr. J. Alden Mason, Curator Emeritus of the American Section of the University Museum, University of Pennsylvania, for reading the manuscript. We hasten to add that the authors alone are responsible for any errors of fact or interpretation that may persist in the book.

Dr. Frederick J. Dockstader, Director of the Museum of the American Indian, Heye Foundation, helped in many ways, and he has our warm thanks. Dr. Fred Wendorf of the Laboratory of Anthropology, Santa Fe, New Mexico, and Glenn A. Black, Archaeological Field Director, Indiana Historical Society, made it possible for us to watch digs in progress, and for this we are grateful.

For a wide variety of courtesies we wish to express our indebtedness to the following: C. H. Armstrong, State Parks Superintendent of Oregon; Carroll A. Burroughs of the National Park Service; Mrs. Philip D. Caesar of the New Jersey Archeological Society; Lewis A. Carter of the Massachusetts Department of Natural Resources; Sally M. Clark of the New Jersey State Museum Film Library; Carl B. Compton of the Instituto Interamericano, Denton, Texas; Dr. John Cotter of the National Park Service; Albert H. Culverwell of the Washington State Parks and Recreation Commission; Dr. Bertha Dutton of the Museum of New Mexico; the Eastern States Archeological Federation; Dr. Gordon Ekholm of the American Museum of Natural History; Albert G. Ely of the Museum of New Mexico; Helen R. Gordon of the Rochester (New York) Museum of Arts and Sciences; Kathryn B. Greywacz, Director of the New Jersey State Museum; Wendell S. Hadlock of the William A. Farnsworth Library and Art Museum, Rockland, Maine; Aline T. Havens of the New Hampshire State Planning and Development Commission; Elizabeth Howell of the American Association of Museums; Dr. Wesley R. Hurt of the State University of South Dakota; Joseph Jaeger, Jr., of the Missouri State Park Board; Dr. Jesse D. Jennings of the Department of Anthropology, University of Utah; Mary Gregory Jewett of the Georgia Historical Commission; Marvin F. Kivett of the Nebraska State Historical Society; Warren B. Kuhn of the Princeton University Library; A. F. Lorton, Jr., of the Pacific Northwest Pipeline Corp.; Charles R. Lally of the West Virginia Archeological Society; Kermit McKeever of the West Virginia Conservation Commission; George Metcalfe of the Smithsonian Institution; H. Kirkland Osoinach of the Tennessee Department of Conservation and Commerce; Charles C. Pratt of the Ohio Historical Society; Shirley Ramsey of the Iowa State Conservation Commission; Russell Reid of the State Historical Society of North Dakota; Francis A. Riddell of the California Department of Natural Resources; Martha A. Rolingson of the Museum of Anthropology, University of Kentucky; William F. Ryan of the Rhode Island Division of Parks and Recreation; Dick Shutler, Jr., of the Nevada State Museum; William Smith of the National Park Service; Harry O. Sorensen of the Michigan Department of Conservation; Bryan Stearns of the Arkansas Publicity and Parks Commission; S. K. Stevens of the Pennsylvania Historical and Museum Commission; Dr. Earl H. Swanson of the Idaho State College Museum; Raymond S. Sivesind of the Wisconsin State Historical Society; W. S. Tarlton of the North Carolina Department of Archives and History; Dee C. Taylor of the Department of Anthropology, Montana State University; William A. Wells of the Louisiana State Parks and Recreation Commission. And to Lore Phillips thanks for her patience in getting the manuscript typed.

On page 146 we have noted some books and magazines which we believe parents, teachers and young people will find useful for further reading. We are indebted to all of these publications and to many other works as well. We want particularly to mention the following: the publications of the American Museum of Natural History; of the Bureau of American Ethnology; of the Carnegie Institution; of the Field Museum of Natural History; of the Peabody Museum of American Archaeology and Ethnology; of the University Museum, University of Pennsylvania; ARCHAEOLOGY OF EASTERN UNITED STATES, edited by James B. Griffin; PAINTED CAVE by Emil W. Haury; THE ARCHAEOLOGICAL HIS-

TORY OF NEW YORK by Arthur C. Parker; ANCIENT MEXICO by Frederick A. Peterson; TRACES OF EARLY MAN IN THE NORTHEAST by W. A. Ritchie; ANCIENT CIVILIZATIONS OF MEXICO AND CENTRAL AMERICA by H. J. Spinden; PERU: *Incidents of Travel and Exploration in the Land of the Incas* by E. G. Squier; THE AMERICAN INDIAN by Clark Wissler; ANCIENT MAN IN NORTH AMERICA and PREHISTORIC INDIANS OF THE SOUTHWEST by H. M. Wormington; various issues of the magazines *American Anthropologist, The Masterkey, Plateau, Scientific American.*

And finally a word of gratitude to the men and women of the National Park Service, the many archeologists, rangers, naturalists and guides whose imagination and endless interest in their subject first brought ancient Americans to life for us and our children, as for so many other Park visitors.

Mary Elting
Franklin Folsom

15
Pronouncing Index

Numerals in *Italics* refer to pictures or to subjects mentioned in captions for pictures or for maps.